Contents

Acknowledgments

A book such as this would not be possible if not for the dedicated work of many researchers in the field of marital therapy. In particular, I am most grateful for the research conducted by Dr. John Gottman and Dr. Howard Markman, whose work has inspired me and whose research findings are well represented on these pages.

Thanks again to my literary agent, Mike Snell, whose talent, enthusiasm, and bluefish paté are second to none.

Many thanks for the fine work by the editors at Adams Media, notably Danielle Chiotti.

To my friend Dr. Foster Malmed, who never fails to crack me up.

To my longtime friends Norb and Gail Gottschling, Dr. Arnie Morgan and Alycia Morgan, Dr. Mike Leahy, and Deni O'Hara.

To Tony and Kate Burdick who are role models for many on how to make your marriage not only happy, but sacred.

Of course, many thanks to my wife Jody for her love and encouragement.

And a special thanks to Luke, Anna, and Julia, who reminded me of my priorities when they insisted I read them a story instead of write.

What's New and Exciting in This Updated Version?

About a dozen years have passed since I first wrote *The 30 Secrets of Happily Married Couples*. During that time, new research findings have changed the way many counselors conduct relationship therapy. Therapy today is much more active, and therapists have changed some of their ideas on what really makes a relationship work. For instance:

Old Myth: Shutting down and running away from an argument is never helpful.
New Finding: If agitation is high, a strategic timeout from an argument is essential—as long as the discussion continues when participants are calmer.

Old Myth: Happy couples show much more positive emotions when they interact (humor, affection, agreement, and so on) than do unhappy couples.
New Finding: In a study of newlyweds, couples who later divorced or felt miserable together showed only thirty seconds

per day less positive emotion than their happier counterparts. But the happier couples used those extra thirty seconds like a precision laser beam in the service of de-escalating conflict.

Old Myth: Couples who avoid conflict are suppressing their real feelings and building resentments.
New Finding: Couples who try to avoid arguments at all costs can actually be very happy together. However, if a conflict-avoider is paired with someone who is emotionally volatile, unhappiness will result.

Old Myth: If you cannot resolve your differences you are doing something wrong and the relationship is at risk for failure.
New Finding: Every couple has several permanently irresolvable differences because of personality styles and values. Happy couples learn to manage those differences, not eradicate them.

Old Myth: Major differences in personality account for why some couples are unhappy together.
New Finding: Personality differences do not predict marital success or failure. It is each partner's perception and interpretation of those personality traits that make the most difference.

Old Myth: It is important to make "I" statements, not "You" statements, when communicating ("*I* felt hurt when you teased me in front of our friends" as opposed to "*You* were wrong to tease me in front of our friends").
New Finding: "I" statements are unnatural and hard to do under stress. Happy couples find other ways to communicate effectively.

As a result of those and other new findings, I eliminated over half of the original "secrets" and replaced them with brand new insights. All of the remaining chapters have been completely updated and expanded.

Part One reveals fifteen *positive* steps couples should take to *increase* marital quality. It lists the key actions and attitudes that couples need to *do more* of to improve marital joy. Part Two lists the fifteen *negative* behaviors and attitudes that must be *reduced*. Reducing negative interactions and increasing positive ones is vitally important in a marriage—but for different reasons. Negative behaviors and attitudes must be reduced because they are costly. One negative interaction—even a small argument or a misperception—costs between five and ten positive interactions. However, couples that break many of the new relationship rules will survive if their ratio of positive to negative interactions is at least 5:1 according to Dr. John Gottman at the University of Washington. If a couple manages to have few negative moments but few positive ones as well, the marriage may feel a little flat. Positive interactions give life to a relationship.

If you've already read the previous edition of this book I'm sure you'll be pleased at the multitude of new tips and strategies you will now have at your disposal. To the new readers I say thanks for putting your faith in me. This book won't let you down.

Paul Coleman, Psy.D.

Take the Happiness Test

Have you ever been to a restaurant and noticed (perhaps with envy and a bit of nostalgia) that couple who seem just crazy about each other? Those romantics who devise ways to hold hands during the appetizer, lay bare their souls in intimate conversation over dinner, smile warmly and tenderly throughout the evening, and generally gaze upon one another with rapture?

Those were the days. Remember? You don't have to be unhappy in your marriage to wish it could be happier. You can have a committed, caring relationship but still be weary of complacency, frustrated with your partner's personality quirks, and secretly wondering, "Wouldn't it be wonderful if he'd only . . ."

You can have a good marriage but discover during times of stress and adversity that your relationship has its weak spots.

You can have a good marriage but as you lie next to your partner at night still sense a muted stirring of discontentment, a restlessness in your heart . . . a quiet realization that you're not as happy as you need to be and that some relationship changes are in order.

When you get right down to it, better communication or more creative sex isn't all you want. It's ultimately marital happiness—marital joy—that you're seeking. And most of us want more because we believe deep down that more joy is not only possible but *necessary* for a worthwhile life together.

So how do you transform a troubled relationship into a satisfying one? And how do you make a satisfactory marriage even happier? Answering those questions is what this book is all about.

Just How Happy Are We in Our Marriages?

Conventional wisdom goofed.

As the divorce rate rose in the eighties and nineties, it was commonly predicted that the average level of satisfaction for intact marriages would automatically improve—the "unhappiest" couples had divorced and were no longer bringing down the overall average.

In the past twenty years, measures of "happiness" in marriages have remained unchanged—and in some studies, declined slightly—despite the fact that the most unhappy couples have (presumably) divorced. What is going on in marriages with this thing called "happiness"?

One of the best-designed studies of marital happiness, conducted by the Gallup organization, reported that about 60 percent of the respondents rated their marriage as "very happy. Yet of those "very happy" people, only 66 percent reported that their spouse respected their opinion. Only 64 percent of the "very happy" said their spouse made them feel important. Only 51 percent felt their spouse was romantic. When you add to these numbers the fact that almost 35 percent of couples rated their marriage as just "pretty happy," and that 37 percent of all women polled admitted there was a time when they were prepared to leave their husband, it becomes obvious that in the typical marriage, genuine happiness seems . . . blunted.

But so what? Is subdued marital happiness such a big deal? Absolutely. Dozens of research studies have concluded that the best predictor of overall happiness in life is marital happiness. (A happy marriage predicts overall happiness better than does job satisfaction, family life, friendships, finances, or good health.) Happily married people live longer, have better-adjusted children, and are healthier psychologically and physically. In one analysis of more than 18,000 people from thirty-nine countries, women were happier than men, and married women were the happiest of all (followed by married men, unmarried women, and unmarried men).

Do people strive and hope for more happiness in their marriage? Most couples report regular efforts to sustain and improve marital satisfaction. When asked in a Gallup survey, "If you had to do it all over again, would you marry the same person?" 88 percent said "yes." But astoundingly, 26 percent of those "mostly dissatisfied" in their marriage also answered "yes," as did 23 percent of those "completely dissatisfied" (as reported in the book *Rebuilding the Nest*). It is unclear why, but many Americans (die-hard romantics?) don't want to give up when it comes to their marriage—even if the marriage is making them unhappy.

Does one's level of marital happiness predict who will eventually divorce? Not quite. It appears that those who are most happy are very unlikely to divorce, but many unhappy couples do remain together. Thus, a clear benefit to improving marital happiness is to reduce the risk of divorce in some cases and to improve the quality of family life for those couples that might remain together anyway.

Age and Happiness

Researcher Lynn White at the University of Nebraska showed that because of fewer social barriers to divorce, as well as more alternatives to current partners (especially available when you are younger), youthful couples don't have to be miserable before they seek out divorce. In other words, for today's couples, especially younger ones, higher levels of marital satisfaction are required to keep the couple together. This is consistent with the decades-long findings that half of all divorces will occur within the first seven years of marriage. Young couples in particular need help in strengthening their marriages during their earliest years so they can weather the storms (adjusting to a new extended family; climbing a career ladder; raising children; investing in property; and so forth) most common among newlyweds.

What Makes a Happy Marriage Happy?

Is your spouse kind, trustworthy, gentle, a skilled lover, good with the kids, and helpful around the house? Having a spouse who fits that bill may seem ideal to some, yet these factors account for only 50 percent of happiness in a marriage. Happiness is elusive. It is not a goal you can directly attain.

Rather, it appears to be a by-product of living a caring, loving, moral, and accomplished life—and even then you can be unhappy from time to time. Certain events can make you feel happy (a birth of a child, a romantic anniversary gift, the bigger and better house or car) but it really is true that day-to-day happiness fluctuates.

How Happy Are You, Really?

The following quiz will give you some idea of where your relationship stands when it comes to achieving happiness. Check the answer that seems closest to how you feel.

1. When we're apart I think fondly about my partner.
   Mostly True _____ *Sometimes True* _____ *Mostly False* _____

2. Arguments with my partner tend to escalate with no satisfying resolution.
   Mostly True _____ *Sometimes True* _____ *Mostly False* _____

3. I admire my partner.
   Mostly True _____ *Sometimes True* _____ *Mostly False*_____

4. At least one of us has a problem with addiction(s) (alcohol, drugs, gambling, pornography).
   Mostly True _____ *Sometimes True* _____ *Mostly False*_____

5. If my partner says or does something I don't like, I don't view him or her as having a serious flaw.
   Mostly True _____ *Sometimes True* _____ *Mostly False*_____

6. My partner frequently says or does mean and hurtful things.
    Mostly True _____ *Sometimes True* _____ *Mostly False* _____

7. We have at least twenty minutes a day of quality "couple time."
    Mostly True _____ *Sometimes True* _____ *Mostly False* _____

8. Much of the time, things have to go my partner's way.
    Mostly True _____ *Sometimes True* _____ *Mostly False* _____

9. Each of us can admit it when we're wrong.
    Mostly True _____ *Sometimes True* _____ *Mostly False* _____

10. I'm dissatisfied with our sexual relationship.
    Mostly True _____ *Sometimes True* _____ *Mostly False* _____

11. We show affection regularly.
    Mostly True _____ *Sometimes True* _____ *Mostly False* _____

12. I fantasize about leaving my partner for someone else.
    Mostly True _____ *Sometimes True* _____ *Mostly False* _____

For odd-numbered statements, score five points for "Mostly True"; three points for "Sometimes True"; and score one point for "Mostly False." For even-numbered statements, score one point for "Mostly True"; three points for "Sometimes True"; and score five points for "Mostly False."

50–60: Your relationship is probably very happy and satisfying with perhaps one or two areas in need of mild improvement.

40–49: Your relationship is probably happy or somewhat happy. However, you need to make improvements in several areas.

28–39: Your relationship is probably "comfortable" at best with some moderate happiness experienced occasionally. Time to upgrade your marriage.

20–27: Your relationship is not very satisfying. You may have moments of contentment but mostly you are not happy and are probably depressed. Make improvements now before it's too late.

19 or below: You are very unhappy in your relationship. Improvements are unlikely without professional help.

How to Use This Book

The recommended exercises you'll find in this book are not complicated. They are designed to bring about rapid change (from a few hours to a few weeks). While many are designed for partners to perform together, most can be done without the knowledge of your spouse, although cooperation is very helpful. Some interventions will be more useful to your particular needs than other interventions. If you find the exercises or techniques aren't as effective as you'd hoped, consider the following:

Have you applied the techniques properly and consistently? Some people give up too quickly on exercises. Most are intended to be tried numerous times over many weeks.

Are your expectations for change realistic? Most changes in behavior will be punctuated by backslides once in a while. And once positive changes do occur, developing them into habit requires additional effort. Marriages with very serious problems (alcoholism or other addictions, abusiveness, etc.) require specialized treatment in addition to marital therapy.

Have you identified the real problem? For example, sometimes a sexual problem is really a communication problem; or sometimes stubbornness derives from a belief that one's feelings haven't been taken seriously in the past.

Have you or your partner sought the services of a divorce lawyer? If so, the marital problems are serious and commitment to the marriage is halfhearted at best. Talking with a qualified marital therapist will be a necessary step.

Did You Know?

A happy marriage can profoundly affect your physical health. In one study, 10,000 Israeli men were evaluated to see who would develop angina pectoris—a condition wherein the blood supply to the heart is reduced. Amazingly, men who answered yes to the question, "Does your wife show you her love?" were two times *less likely* to develop angina than men who responded no.

Researcher Janice Kiecolt-Glaser at Ohio State University School of Medicine measured the immune-system functioning of married women. Immune functioning was better for women in satisfying marriages than for women in unsatisfying marriages (or for women recently separated or divorced.)

No doubt about it, marital dissatisfaction increases one's odds of becoming physically ill.

Are other extramarital difficulties affecting you? If you or your mate is currently coping with a health, family, or career problem, the ability to deal effectively with the marriage may be compromised.

This book is designed so that you can begin at any chapter you wish. You don't have to read through earlier chapters in order to better understand the later ones. The chapter titles that catch your eye are probably good indicators of where your relationship needs improving (and remember: No one has a perfect relationship).

I believe it is very possible to dramatically boost the quality and satisfaction of your relationship. Most of the material in this book is based on state-of-the-art research and the remainder is based upon my twenty-plus years of experience as a relationship therapist.

It's your marriage, your future, your happiness, and your family's happiness, at stake when you commit to a marriage. You and your family deserve to make your marriage the best it can be.

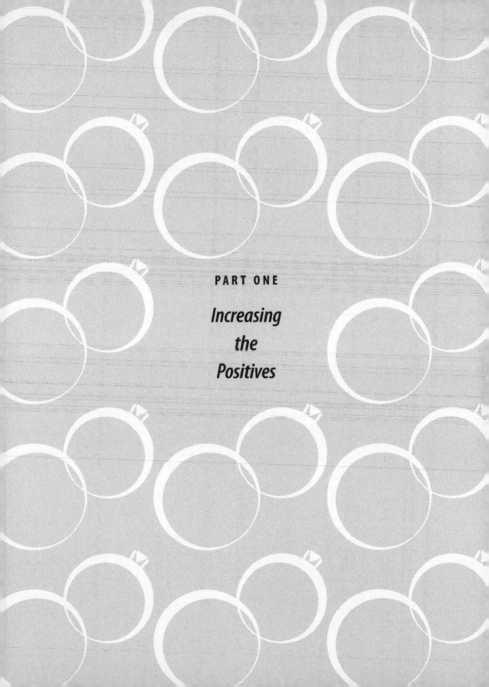

PART ONE

*Increasing
the
Positives*

Secret #1

Tap into the Hurricane-Force Power of Small Talk

The evening was drawing to a close. Bill sat in his favorite chair flipping through the cable channels. Jane was preparing for bed. "Oh, how did your meeting with the finance team go today," Jane said. "I forgot to ask you earlier."

"Same-old, same-old," Bill said.

"But I thought this meeting was crucial," Jane persisted.

"I never said it was crucial. It was just a meeting. No big deal." Bill turned the volume up on the TV.

"My mistake, I guess." Jane looked at him quizzically. "Are you all right?"

When Bill didn't respond, Jane said, "I asked if you were—Oh, never mind."

She left the room, annoyed and rightly so. She wasn't interested in a long discussion. She just wanted to chat briefly and to show interest in Bill's life! Sure, Bill had the right to not want to talk. Perhaps he was tired. Still, it wouldn't have taken much to answer her questions with a little more enthusiasm.

The next day, the couple received a wedding invitation. It was from one of Bill's high school friends. The wedding date was the day before they were to leave for their summer vacation. Jane wanted to skip the wedding because they would be too busy preparing for their trip. Bill wanted to attend the **> > >**

>>> wedding. Within a minute their discussion became heated and then turned into an argument.

Neither Jane nor Bill realized that their argument had a lot to do with the failed attempt at small talk the night before.

The Magic of Chitchat

One of the more fascinating research findings of the past decade is that couples who have regular, pleasant conversations about ordinary, uncontroversial issues are less likely to turn a small disagreement later on into a big fight. In contrast, when one partner displays negativity during everyday chitchat, the stage is set for a bigger argument later. Pleasant chitchat can act as a buffer against future relationship problems. Just like Vitamin C might protect you from a cold virus, small talk with your partner protects you from unnecessary arguments.

Small talk does not require intimate self-disclosure—although it might. Small talk is often simply chatting about your day, the kids, your weekend plans, the weather, minor aggravations at work, neighborhood gossip, and so on. Couples have these conversations practically every day, but happy couples take full advantage of those moments. In particular, they make sure to have a reasonably pleasant, cooperative attitude and display some kind of warmth toward each other. Less than happy couples have these chats but one partner is in a cranky mood, mumbles uncooperatively, or generally seems impatient. The key difference is the pleasant, cooperative demeanor inherent in happy couples' small talk.

It makes sense that these small, routine conversations pack a wallop. Because the talks are short and about uncontroversial topics, partners can expect cooperation. When a partner doesn't get it, he may feel dismissed or not cared about. A partner might think, "Gee, if we can't even talk about the small stuff how can we ever talk about the bigger things?"

Couples these days are busier than ever. Small talk is often the only chance during the week to connect with each other. When small talk doesn't happen, partners will get crankier. Crankiness leads to avoidance of one another, and avoidance leads to emotional eruptions later on. When small talk happens fairly regularly and tends to go well, each partner feels more connected and cared for. The relationship has a cozier feel, like a pair of warm slippers. Those feelings linger long after the chitchat has ended and make it more likely that a disagreement later on will remain small and nondisruptive.

Small-Talk Rules for Nontalkers

Small talk can still be about important topics. However, the topics shouldn't be controversial or "hot." That means anything that could potentially result in one partner getting upset, angry, or confrontational is off-limits.

It's always valuable when you open up about how you feel. There is a huge difference between saying, "I'm in charge of a new project at work," and, "I'm in charge of a new project at work *and I'm really excited about it.*" People who have a hard time self-disclosing or who just don't talk much will often keep "feeling" words to themselves. They might convey the facts about their day or some issues, but they won't convey their feelings about those facts.

If you are not one for small talk or you tend to keep your feelings about things to yourself during conversations, tossing in a few "feeling" words can turn the small talk into something more magical. Your partner wants to continue to know you. When you omit how you feel, you are shutting yourself off from people who care about you. That will kill intimacy over time. Participate effectively in chitchat by injecting some "feeling" words into your everyday conversations. You don't have to elaborate much at all, and the conversation can be brief.

As for responses to your partner's small talk, even the occasional "That's nice" or "Uh-huh" or "Sounds interesting" phrases are better than no response at all.

When you're not usually the one to make small talk, try following these guidelines.

- Aim for at least twenty minutes a day of pleasant chitchat. Fifteen of those minutes should come in one sitting: dinnertime, right before bedtime, first thing upon awakening, and so on.
- Don't roll your eyes, show impatience, or mumble incoherently as a way to end the discussion.
- Try to physically touch at various points during the small talk. Keep it tender.
- Don't make sexual advances during this time. If you must make advances, wait until the small talk is finished.

● Give compliments during this time.

● Use "feeling words" once in a while.

● Don't feel pressured to have a constant discussion. Pauses with little to say are okay as long as the two of you are still connecting in some way.

Small-Talk Rules for Big Talkers

If you have an easy time chatting and expressing your feelings, making small talk will seem like a breeze—but be careful. Big talkers can have a way of turning pleasant small talk into cumbersome conversations. Your goal is to connect with your mate with *light* conversation, not dominate. If you talk more than your mate, follow these guidelines to keep your chitchat charming.

● Don't turn small talk into "bitching" sessions. You have a right to complain about whatever you need to, but allow time during the day for small talk to be light and pleasant.

● Don't ask questions that require yes or no or one-word responses. Instead, make open-ended comments. "How was your day?" is not as effective as "Tell me about your day," or, "Tell me what your mother said when she called."

● Occasionally, let your partner know how much these small talks mean to you.

● Try to make small talk while sitting or lying down, preferably together. If one of you is standing up or walking around, this increases the odds of a premature exit.

● Small talk can be nonverbal. Cuddling while relaxing on a couch or listening to music, interspersed with occasional chitchat is quite fine.

What to Do

☑ *Keep it informal.* Don't feel obligated to have small talks that are serious and proper. A great way to have chitchats that don't make either one of you feel self-conscious is to talk while one of you is giving the other a back rub, foot rub, or body massage. The one doing the rubbing can be the main talker, perhaps chatting about your day. Then switch places.

Or, go for a stroll while chatting. This will allow you opportunity to make pleasant commentary about the weather, neighborhood, etc. Again, talking need not be continuous because there may not be much to talk about on any given day.

☑ *Discover the usefulness of "pitching back."* When your partner is speaking but you don't have much to say, use pitch-backs. Offer a short phrase or sentence that shows interest on your part, without your having to carry on your side of the conversation. Simple—and sincere!—phrases such as "That's interesting . . . Uh-huh . . . Tell me more . . . How did that make you feel?" and so forth are very helpful. Cue in to any emotion-packed word that your partner uses. Once you hear it, pitch back your understanding of what your partner was feeling, such as "That must have made you angry," "You must have been thrilled," "You sound excited."

☑ *Have thirty-second "power" conversations.* A power conversation adds a jolt of intimacy and caring into a small segment of time. For example, asking what's for dinner is a neutral comment. But showing some affection while asking the same question and continuing with a follow-up comment or two—"Oh, that's my favorite!"—adds a little spice and coziness to what ordinarily would have been a throw-away moment.

Keep in Mind

♡ Twenty minutes a day of pleasant small talk with your partner adds intimacy to your relationship and protects it from unnecessary arguments later on.

♡ Small talk should not be about controversial topics. Keep it light.

♡ If you can make small talk into a ritual, all the better.

♡ Small talk isn't mostly about conveying information—it's about connecting.

Give the Benefit of the Doubt

Rick came back into the house, clearly in a bad mood, "Where's the phone-book?" When he couldn't locate it immediately he complained further, "Why isn't it always kept in the same place?"

"What's wrong?" Denise said.

"The riding mower won't start. It's hardly a month old! And where is the phonebook! I have to call that garden equipment place and find out what they intend to do about this."

"I'll find it," Denise said. "It's around here somewhere."

"Nothing's ever where it should be in this house."

"Take it easy. I'll find the book."

Denise didn't get angry at Rick's outburst but she could have. After all, it wasn't her fault the mower wasn't working and his tone was on the nasty side. And his remark about things not being in their place was an unfair jab. Still, Denise kept her cool. It was a small incident but it spoke volumes as to why their relationship was a happy one.

Denise gave Rick the benefit of the doubt when he was in an angry mood. And that's what made all the difference.

Imagine that you and your mate arranged to meet for an hour-long lunch. You don't have an opportunity to do that often, so it will be a special day. Your partner calls your cell phone to say he'll be about ten minutes late because he was delayed with a client. You're annoyed that lunch will be cut short. But the real question is this: Will you view his lateness as a result of some character flaw and lack of consideration; or will you view it as due to extenuating circumstances? Will you give your partner the benefit of the doubt or doubt the benefits of your partner?

Esteemed researcher John Gottman, at the University of Washington, refers to this as "positive sentiment override," whereby your positive feelings about your partner override his negative actions. It doesn't mean you will tolerate abusive behaviors or pretend that obnoxious behaviors are perfectly acceptable. Positive sentiment override, or giving the benefit of the doubt, is a willingness to cut your partner some slack when he's not being very nice or sensitive. When you give the benefit of the doubt, you recognize that your partner's attitude or behavior isn't ideal and is perhaps hurtful. And you may even tell him to stop. But you are also able to look past his actions and tell yourself that he is still a pretty good person.

"Negative sentiment override" is the opposite: Your negative feelings about a partner override his neutral (neither good nor bad) actions. Usually this happens in relationships where one person is insecure and mistrusting to begin with, or where the couple has drifted apart and ill will outweighs goodwill. When this occurs, even a somewhat positive action by a partner can be interpreted negatively. For example, when Jill discovered that her husband, Frank, had washed and vacuumed her car without being asked, she was not happy or grateful. She and Frank had not been getting along for many months. Her first thought when she saw her shining, clean car was "He only did that so I'd have sex with him tonight." She may have been right. But he still washed her car and did her a favor, for which she should feel appreciation.

Failing to give the benefit of the doubt will make a good relationship go sour, and a sour relationship become intolerable. Giving the benefit of the doubt makes a good relationship better and a weak relationship stronger.

If you're like most people, you tend to give the benefit of the doubt at least initially. It's only when the relationship has fallen into a rut or there have been too many misunderstandings or the two of you just haven't been getting along that negative sentiment override creeps in.

❔ Did You Know?

The more ill will you have toward your partner, the less you will be able to accurately assess why your partner is being negative, and the more likely it is you will believe that your assessment is accurate. If you continue to interpret a partner's actions in the most negative light, a self-fulfilling prophecy will occur. Your partner will probably become more negative, more vindictive, more secretive, or more underhanded in response to your ways. If you want your relationship to last and be satisfying, you must be willing to interpret your partner's actions in a less negative light.

Also, research findings show that when a couple is not getting along, they under-detect by as much as 50 percent a partner's positive actions. Emphasizing the negative and de-emphasizing the positive can only make the situation worse.

Make Sure You Have the Benefit of the Doubt, Too

Some people have a hard time giving anybody the benefit of the doubt—friends, family, neighbors, coworkers, and so on. Other people might be able to give a friend or coworker the benefit of the doubt, but not a spouse. People in the first category tend to be suspicious of others to begin with, and they often have a history of having been betrayed or let down by family or friends. They view people as having ulterior motives and they find it hard to forgive and forget. They also tend to be controlling in their relationships. Sometimes, an overly accommodating partner might try to prove trustworthiness by submitting to the suspicious partner's ways. Over time, that submissive partner feels imprisoned and the suspicious spouse hasn't become more trusting. If you are trustworthy, and a person of goodwill, but your partner repeatedly accuses you of being untrustworthy and you are not given the benefit of the doubt, your relationship will never be a satisfying one unless your partner changes. Then you need to be both firm and encouraging. Be firm by stating that you won't tolerate any more false accusations. But be encouraging by thanking your partner when he treats you fairly and showing him that the two of you can have a quality relationship when you are treated respectfully and without suspiciousness.

Key Attitude Shifts

When it is apparent that you are not giving your partner the benefit of the doubt, it's time to make these four shifts in attitude:

1. *If my partner is angry or in a bad mood, it must be because something is troubling him that he thinks is important.* In the opening example, Rick was in a bad mood because his riding mower wasn't working. Denise looked past his grumpy demeanor and realized that he was upset because they had spent a lot of money on the mower. Also, he didn't have a lot of time to do the necessary yard work and now he would be delayed. She attributed his crankiness to extenuating circumstances.

2. *My partner's bad mood might be due to outside factors that have nothing to do with me or our relationship.* Don't take it personally. People get cranky when they are hot, tired, hungry, feeling sick, or overworked. Look for those possible reasons the next time your spouse is a grump. You can still speak up and tell your spouse to show more consideration, but be willing to attribute his actions more to stress, ill health, or outside forces than to a character flaw.

3. *My interpretation of my partner's actions may have to do with the mood I'm in at the time.* If you're in a sour mood (and if you are, you have very good reasons, right?) then you might view your spouse in a more negative light. Ask yourself, "If I was feeling happier right now, would I be able to view my partner more favorably?" If so, it's your mood, not your spouse's that needs improvement.

4. *My partner and I might be caught up in a vicious cycle.* It might be that your spouse meant to be insensitive or malicious. But if he did so in response to your unkind actions—which were a response to being treated

unkindly, as well—then the two of you are trapped in a pattern. Recognize that you are getting nowhere and put a halt to the skirmishes. From there, try to rebuild the relationship by going out of your way to be more thoughtful to one another.

Give the Benefit of the Doubt—But Don't Be a Fool

It's important to repeat that giving the benefit of the doubt means that you judge your partner's motives less harshly or more benignly. It doesn't mean you must repeatedly put up with nasty behaviors. If you cut your partner slack when he continues to act in toxic ways, you are hurting yourself and the relationship. Some behaviors you can look past and put up with, at least occasionally. But some are destructive. If any of the following situations apply to you, you need to take a clearer stand on what is and what is not acceptable if you want to have a chance at happiness:

- Any action that is emotionally, verbally, or physically abusive. Emotional abuse includes such things as being made to feel you're worthless or crazy, having to put up with unpredictable outbursts, and living in fear. Verbal abuse includes insults and name-calling, being yelled at frequently and for no reason, and remarks that make you feel stupid or worthless. Physical abuse can include things like pushing or restraining you, in addition to striking you.
- Any addictive behavior or habit, be it drugs, alcohol, gambling, sex, etc.

- Controlling or possessive behaviors. This includes restricting where you go and whom you see, false accusations, and having to submit to the other's wishes.
- Infidelity. This can include an "emotional affair" where sex is not a part of the picture but infatuation and secrecy is. It also includes Internet relationships where the talk gets sexy and the content of those discussions is kept secret from you.

If you are unsure whether to tolerate certain behaviors that hurt you, speak to close friends or family whose opinion you trust, along with a counselor or member of the clergy. If the consensus is that you are being mistreated, take that opinion seriously.

What to Do

☑ *For one week, make a running list of everything your partner does that is the least bit positive.* Don't overlook a positive action by saying to yourself, "He should do that anyway." A positive action is a positive action. You will be amazed at how many things you don't give your partner credit for. Remember: You are actually under-reporting your partner's positive actions, because you were not around all the time to observe everything. Also, many positive actions go undetected because they are nonactions: A partner *doesn't* say something unkind when he felt like it; a partner *doesn't* show anger or frustration when it is felt; or a partner goes along with something—without letting you know—that he would rather not have gone along with.

☑ *When your partner does something you don't like, ask yourself, "If I did the same thing, might I have a good reason?"* We often find reasons to justify our own negative behaviors. Can we do the same for our partner?

☑ *Say thanks when your partner gives you the benefit of the doubt.* If you're in a bad mood and your partner is very sympathetic, despite the fact that you've been no fun to be around, show appreciation. Say, "Sorry for being in a bad mood today. Thanks for being so understanding." Your partner will welcome your gratitude and give you the benefit of the doubt in the future.

Keep in Mind

♡ Happy couples will often consider a partner's negative actions in a neutral and somewhat forgiving light.

♡ Unhappy couples will sometimes view a partner's neutral actions as negative.

♡ Unhappy couples will under-detect a partner's positive actions by as much as 50 percent.

♡ Giving the benefit of the doubt does not mean you must tolerate abusive or toxic behaviors.

♡ Show appreciation when you are given the benefit of the doubt.

Magical Attentiveness

Jim comes home late from work. He greets his wife, Janet, warmly; she responds a bit stiffly. "I knew you were going to be too busy today, so I picked up your dry-cleaning for you," he says. "And here is a bottle of wine. I was hoping we could enjoy a glass together after the kids go to sleep." Janet gives a slight nod in Jim's direction, hardly acknowledging him, mumbles "Thanks," and without even a smile directs her attention back to the rambunctious children. Not saying another word, Jim puts the wine in the refrigerator.

Knowing nothing else about this couple, would you guess there was some underlying conflict or problem in this relationship? If so, you've probably bought into the myth that happy couples are quick to show gratitude and appreciation.

Actually, Jim and Janet have a happy marriage. Happy couples with young children are less likely to react immediately and positively to a partner's kindness. The positive reaction may never even come, but some caring or considerate action eventually will. The partners know that and therefore don't feel neglected or unappreciated. They can tolerate the wait.

Unhappy couples are different. Their satisfaction in the marriage is closely tied to the "What have you done for me lately?" attitude. They are much more likely than happy couples to have a strong, *immediate* emotional reaction (positive or negative) to their partner's actions. Learning to give to one's spouse without automatically expecting appreciation is a task for couples wanting to be more satisfied in their marriage. But that only happens when, deep down, a spouse knows his partner cares.

Caring about Caring

Even couples in love wake up some mornings not feeling in love. The emotion of love often comes in waves. Some days you know it's "out there" but it hasn't yet rolled in to greet you—and that's okay. But that normal occurrence frightens couples that are having marital problems. They wonder if not feeling in love means they've fallen *out* of love. When the feeling of love has receded, it's important to focus on caring. You can care without loving, but there is no love without caring. The knowledge—the experience—of being cared about by a partner often deepens commitment, inspires intimacy, and sparks passion.

When a couple successfully ends marriage therapy, I often ask them "What worked? What made the biggest difference in resolving your differences?" Roberta's answer was typical: "Finally believing that Steve understood—no, more than that—believing he *cared* about my feelings even if he disagreed with me. That's what made it work for me."

Happier couples care about caring.

Caring: Money in the Relationship Bank

When your bank account is nearly empty, every deposit or withdrawal is keenly felt. In relationships, every act of love or caring is like money in the relationship bank. Each argument or instance of uncaring is like a withdrawal from the account. To be happy, couples must have a reserve of love and caring to help through the rainy days in their relationship.

How much caring is enough? Research findings suggest that a marriage can withstand conflict if the ratio of caring to conflict is at least five to one and perhaps as high as ten to one. The difficulty for severely distressed couples, however, is that an upsurge in caring doesn't automatically erase months or years of anger or unkindness. Commonly, one major argument for a dissatisfied couple can erase the effects of ten to twenty positive interactions. Fortunately, for the average, satisfied couple who wish to boost their overall happiness, daily, random acts of kindness are good medicine.

Most partners *believe* they care, and they'll point to numerous acts they perform every day to prove it. But a funny thing happens on the way to your fifth wedding anniversary: Actions once viewed as considerate and special by an appreciative spouse (filling the gas tank, sewing on a button) are now expected, and sometimes demanded. You don't get credit for doing them anymore. So when the wife exits an important meeting at work to pick up a sick child from school, her husband takes that for granted. And if the husband spends his Saturday installing a shelf-unit, his wife's attitude is, "That's his job. He knows I have no talent for that and God knows we can't afford to hire someone else to do it." Where is the appreciation? (It evaporated at about the same time watching a ball game or "getting a good night's sleep" became more important than having sex.)

Pay Attention to Small Desires for Attention

Caring gestures are obviously important in creating happiness in a relationship. Those small, everyday interactions that couples share may seem insignificant but they are actually incredibly powerful and can sometimes make or break the relationship. A bid for attention is often a small, sometimes hardly noticeable gesture that says, "I'm here. Does it matter?" For many couples it is the foundation of their ability—or inability—to get along. For example, perhaps you are busy working on the computer. Your spouse comes up behind you and kisses you. You notice it but say nothing and just continue working. Or, you ask if your new coat looks nice and your spouse grumbles something incoherent. Or you give your mate a passionate kiss and you get an uninspired kiss in return. All of those bids for attention went *splat*. The good news is that failed bids are very common so you're not alone. No spouse, happy or unhappy, responds favorably to all bids for attention. And in happy relationships it is understood that failed attempts to get attention are usually the result of fatigue or mindless inattention by a partner—not active disinterest or rejection.

Still, you won't feel very friendly and affectionate toward a partner who routinely rejects those small efforts on your part to get attention. In fact, the larger caring gesture such as giving flowers or spending a night out on the town won't mean nearly so much if the smaller caring gestures—favorable responses to bids for attention—go unrewarded.

In addition, failed bids tend to build upon one another. If your desire for attention is met with indifference, the chances increase that you won't respond when your partner seeks your attention. Unless you're careful, such actions can lead to mutual resentment and a distancing from one another.

The solution is to "complete the circuit." If you think of an interaction with your spouse as an electrical circuit, you must respond to a partner's bid for attention to complete the circuit. A simple smile, hand squeeze, or a few words may be all that is necessary to complete the circuit. Bids for attention are usually not demands for a lot of time together. They are small,

? Did You Know?

Marriages made to last are not always fifty-fifty propositions? *Psychology Today* published a survey of 351 couples married for at least fifteen years that stated the happiest among them agreed "You have to be willing to put in more than you take out." At any point in a marriage, such things as a serious illness, job loss, or career change may mean that one partner contributes 80 percent to the marriage for months on end. Happy couples can handle that and don't feel owed by the less involved partner. They trust that in the long run (over months or years) the give-and-take will balance out. In contrast, dissatisfied partners have a "tit-for-tat" approach, one that virtually ensures greater dissatisfaction. (In a five-year study published in the *Journal of Marriage and Family*, spouses who were kind to one another, but only with an "I'll be nice if you are nice" attitude, broke up within five years.)

Are you and your mate willing to put in more than you take out of your relationship with little resentment? Chances are your marriage will last.

quick moments where there is an opportunity to connect. If you increase those moments by responding to a partner's effort to get attention, your overall relationship satisfaction will increase.

When satisfaction is increased it is then easier to give your partner the benefit of the doubt (see **Secret #2**) when he or she is not easy to get along with.

What to Do

☑ *Pinpoint ten to fifteen deeds you already do that you know have a positive impact on your mate.* Then do them more often. Your list might include making a meal for your mate, fixing her a cup of tea without being asked, showing appreciation or affection, vacuuming the interior of her car, meeting him for lunch, having coffee together before you go to work, tidying up, etc.

☑ *Discover new ways to show caring.* Each of you should draw up a list of at least ten small, nonconflicting things a partner could do that would make you feel cared for (i.e., "Kiss me when you get home," "Massage my feet," "Give me fifteen minutes of free time when I first get home from work"). The tasks should be small, inexpensive, and require little time, and they should be very specific. ("Talk more to me" is vague. "Take ten minutes tonight and discuss how our day went" is specific.) The goal is to do two things a day from your partner's list; that is sixty *extra* caring tasks a month. Most important, express thanks every time your partner shows caring. Appreciative comments encourage your mate. Silence may be interpreted as lack of interest or gratitude.

☑ *Have a "politeness week."* One spouse is to treat the other as if he/she were a special guest. (A good host is polite even when a guest is not!) Polite behaviors may include fixing breakfast; asking what the other person would like to watch on television; asking, "Can I get you anything?" as you leave the room to get yourself a snack; and saying "Please," "Thank you," and "Excuse me." Houseguests are often treated with more consideration than family members. A "politeness week" will make you more aware of the small ways you can show more consideration.

☑ *Go the extra mile.* The relationship title *In Quest of the Mythical Mate* suggests that once a week you ask your partner, "What is one thing I could do today (or this week) that would make your day go a little easier or make you feel a bit more special?" This is an opportunity for your mate to express wishes that might be more involved than the ones listed for "caring days." Everyone can fall into a self-absorbed rut. Taking time to ask your partner what would make him or her feel special can help you climb out of that rut.

☑ *Be more responsive when your partner seeks your attention.* Aim to improve your responsiveness by 50 percent. Pay close attention to all of the small bids for attention your partner shows. Make sure you respond favorably, even in a small way, to as many as you can. Pay attention to the number of times you put

off a partner by saying "Not now . . . I'm busy . . . Later . . . "
and so forth. Try to reduce the frequency you say those things
and instead be more responsive more quickly.

Keep in Mind

♡ Happy marriages are not free from conflict, but the conflict
is offset by mutual acts of kindness and respect and by positive feelings toward one's spouse.

♡ Good intentions are nice, but the road to a happy relationship is paved by genuine acts of desired love and caring.

♡ When you doubt your partner really cares about you, all of
his positive acts are suspect. When you believe your partner cares about you, none of his inconsiderate acts are taken
too personally.

♡ If you routinely show disinterest to a partner's attempt to
get some attention, you will undermine the foundation of
your relationship.

♡ If you want to feel more "special," tell your mate ways she
can act that would make you feel that way. She will probably appreciate the guidelines.

Secret #4

Nurture One Another, and Be Good Friends

Eric and Jill sat down for their first therapy session. They have been married fifteen years but the last few had seen them drift farther and farther apart. Jill summarized their difficulties with one sentence that really captured the essence of their problems: "We've stopped nurturing each other."

Nurturing happens in a multitude of ways: how you talk to each other and hear each other out; how you show affection and tenderness; how you inspire one another to reach your dreams; how you care about each other's needs at least as much as you care about your own. Happy couples are good friends, and friends nurture one another.

Somewhere in the marital mix of passion, intimacy, and commitment lies an all-too-forgotten quality: friendship. Usually the friendship aspect of one's marriage gets buried over time, under the burdens and responsibilities of life, work, and family. When asked if they feel like they are friends, the average couple would say yes. But then it gets complicated. They might realize that they don't always treat one another as they would their same-sex friends. They think of having a night out "with friends" as somehow different from a night out "with my spouse." Some couples assume that they must be friends simply because most of the time they act friendly toward one another and they don't think of each other as enemies. But friendship is more than friendliness. (You can be friendly toward a neighbor you rarely see.) Friendship is in many ways the foundation of a marital relationship. Happy couples realize that. Less happy couples usually have forgotten it.

What Does Friendship Mean to You?

Think of someone other than your spouse whom you consider to be your best friend. What is the difference between that friendship and your marriage relationship? Friends talk about their personal lives; so do married partners. Friends have fun together; (hopefully) so do married couples. Friends think about each other when they're not together; married partners do the same. Friends stand by you; so does a spouse. Fundamentally there are two ways a marriage is different than a friendship (at least in theory): You have a greater level of obligation and commitment to your spouse than to your best friend; and you have a sexual relationship with your spouse but not your friend.

The typical man approaches friendship with his wife a little differently than she approaches friendship with him. If you ask a man about his male friendships and what makes them important, he will talk about what he and his friends *do* together—the *interests* they share. Men friends might discuss their personal problems with one another but those conversations are not usually in depth. In contrast, a woman will tell you that *conversation* forms the primary basis of intimacy in her friendships. Doing things with her friends is important, too, but communication— understanding one another and being understood—is essential. If a man has a problem and doesn't want to discuss it, his male friends "understand" that. Ironically, he will feel "understood" and therefore emotionally closer to his friends by *not sharing information*. However, a woman feels emotionally closer to her friends by disclosing personal information and feeling understood and cared about in the process. What does this mean for marriages? It means that, generally speaking, the basis for friendship in a marriage depends on the couple doing more together (a male preference) and talking more together (a female preference).

Talking Like Friends

Secret #1 (Tapping Into the Hurricane-Force Power of Small Talk) is a great place to start if you want to improve the quality of communication and self-disclosure. But talking like friends involves more than small talk. Friends think about one another in a positive way and inquire about each other's lives. A good friend doesn't just say, "How are you?" A good friend listened to previous conversations and recalls certain facts and asks specific questions such as, "How is your mother doing? Is she out of the hospital yet?" or "How did it go at the meeting with your boss?" If you are a good friend you think of your friends often and wonder about specific events in their lives.

Many couples fall short in this area. Their marriage is more "out of sight, out of mind." For example, your spouse has a dentist or medical appointment: Are you likely to remember that during the day? Are you likely to ask about it later? Or maybe your spouse is worried about someone in the extended family: Do you ask about that? Perhaps your partner is on a diet: How often do you inquire how it's going? If your spouse hasn't been feeling well, do you take the time to ask the details of how he or she is feeling? If your partner likes to read books, have you asked about them? Do you know why your spouse likes some books and not others?

To talk like friends you have to make more room in your head for aspects of your spouse's life that you might easily ignore. You might think you know your spouse pretty well but can you answer these questions?

1. What are your spouse's favorite foods? Least favorite?
2. Who would your spouse say is his or her closest same-sex friend?
3. What worries or concerns does your spouse have?
4. What is something your spouse is looking forward to?
5. What is your spouse's favorite time of the day?
6. What hopes and dreams does your spouse still have?
7. Who were your spouse's best childhood friends?
8. What frustrates your spouse most about his or her life?
9. What is your spouse's favorite music? Movie?

The more you know about your spouse, the more you will think about him or her and the more inquiries you will make.

Spending Time Together as Friends

Happiest couples do spend more leisure time together. In one study of 250 people (married an average of twelve years), the best predictor of marital satisfaction was the amount of leisure time spent alone with one's spouse. In particular, wives who spent the least time with their husbands were the most unhappy. But what causes what? Does spending time together create more marital satisfaction, or does marital happiness make couples want to spend more time together?

One researcher interviewed 2,000 couples to determine how spending time together promoted happiness. She speculated that the amount of time together would determine the amount of overall happiness. Her hypothesis was that couples with dual careers, children, and hobbies would spend less time together and consequently be less happy. That wasn't always true. What mostly determined whether couples spent time together was the quality of their marriage. Happier couples wanted to share more time together despite obvious constraints (kids, jobs, and so on).

Sometimes spending a quiet evening cuddled up on the couch together watching a DVD can be very intimate and wonderful, and it adds to a sense of friendship. It's important for couples to have some kind of regular "fun" time together. Otherwise they will get into a rut or grow cranky and restless. You don't have to have date nights every week. You should plan a night together frequently enough that you have something to look forward to.

It's also important to have moments where you really laugh together. Laughing together bonds you in a way that simply spending "nice" time together doesn't. If you think about who your closest friends were throughout your life, they were probably the people who made you laugh.

"Morning" vs. "Night" Partners

Most satisfied partners will tell you that their time alone together is special, that it keeps their friendship alive. Leisure time is at a premium these days, and it's complicated by this fact: One-quarter of all two-income couples do "shift" work. So when the husband works evenings and the wife works days, how do they spend time alone together? And when partners don't work separate shifts, some are mismatched by being a "morning" or a "night" person (a "lark" or an "owl"). Larks love sunrises, breakfast, and the great outdoors and generally feel more energetic the first part of the day. Owls savor sleeping late and nightlife, and they "can't get moving" until the middle of the afternoon.

A 1991 study published in the *Journal of Marital and Family Therapy* showed that mismatched (night versus morning) couples spent less time in shared activities each week (three hours, as opposed to six hours for "matched" couples). And their overall level of satisfaction was lower than that of their counterparts. However, with the right adjustments, owls and larks learned to improve their satisfaction levels.

In order to enjoy more time together, two factors must be present: the *desire* and the *opportunity*. The happiest couples have the desire and make the opportunity.

Must You Be *Best* Friends?

If you and your spouse think of one another as best friends, you are fortunate and probably are very happy together. To think that way about your relationship you must have many things working properly:

- Think fondly and lovingly about one another, especially when the other person is not around.
- Enjoy spending time with each other.
- Share personal feelings and dreams and feel safe (not defensive) doing so.
- Be willing to drop what you're doing and be of service to one another when it's called for.
- Make sacrifices for each other without begrudging it.
- Be very attentive to each other.

While it's okay to have separate interests it's not okay to lead separate lives. You must think the best of each other, not the worst, and cut each other slack when mistakes are made. The relationship must feel fair, not one-sided. You must do what you can to make a partner's dreams come true and nourish each other's self-esteem. It's difficult for even satisfied couples to achieve all of those goals consistently. If you fall short in some areas, does that mean you and your spouse aren't "best friends" after all? Not necessarily. If you think of your closest friends and how you relate to them, you will see that all relationships have their flaws. It has been said that one reason you can be best friends with someone (who is not a spouse) is precisely because you don't have to live with that friend. It is so much easier to be accepting of a friend's quirky ways when you don't have to put up with them day in and day out.

The bottom line is this: Don't focus on whether you and your spouse are best friends. Instead, concentrate on being very solid "good friends" while being willing to make whatever improvements you can in your marital friendship.

What to Do

☑ *Learn as much as you can about your mate in fifteen minutes.* Make it a game. Ask a series of questions as rapidly as possible. How would your spouse spend a million dollars if it could only be spent on himself? What are five things your partner wants to accomplish before he or she dies? Self-disclosure improves intimacy and adds to a sense of friendship.

☑ *Have a "We'll do whatever you want" day.* Your job is to accompany your spouse and do your best to find enjoyment in whatever activities are chosen. Don't be a whiner or a stick in the mud. It helps if your spouse is creative and chooses activities that are special or unique. The underlying goal is to act as a friend and do whatever your spouse wants to do.

☑ *Make minor adjustments to your sleep-wake pattern if one of you is a "night person" and the other is a "morning person,"* as suggested by a study published in the *Journal of Marital and Family Therapy* that researched the effect of wake and sleep patterns on marital adjustment. Staying out a little later than you'd like or rising earlier than you'd prefer is not too much to ask once in a while. A "night" wife shouldn't call her husband boring because he likes to be asleep by 10 P.M. A "morning" husband shouldn't call his wife lazy because she could sleep until noon. If you have an infant, the "night" parent can care for the fussy baby at 1:00 A.M. while the "morning" parent can care for a fussy child at 5:30 A.M. If your children are older, the "morning" spouse can see the kids off to school, the "night" spouse can stay up late waiting for your teenager to arrive home from a date. Show appreciation for *any* changes your spouse makes in her sleep-wake schedule to accommodate you.

Keep in Mind

♡ Friendship is the foundation of any happy marriage.

♡ Friendship in a marriage is more than feeling comfortable with each other; it involves self-disclosure and doing enjoyable things together.

♡ Happy spouses find time for each other despite hectic schedules.

♡ Being best friends in your marriage is wonderful but being good friends will keep you happy, too.

Yield Often to Your Partner's Wishes

Carol and Todd were arguing about whether to use software that will block access to certain Web sites. Carol was worried that their nine-year-old son, Brett, might intentionally or unintentionally log on to pornographic sites and she felt that a blocking device was a must. Todd disagreed. He said he trusted their son, had kept an eye on the situation, and concluded that so far there were no problems. Besides, he feared that blocking devices might interfere with his ability to get onto sites that he needed to access for his job. The argument escalated. Carol said that Todd was selfish and naïve. Todd said Carol was untrusting of their son and stubborn.

When I spoke to them about yielding to one another's wishes they each thought I was crazy. They thought that yielding meant giving in, surrendering, or "backing down when I'm right." Yielding doesn't mean turning yourself into a doormat. It means trying hard to understand a partner's concerns, and seeking common ground. The opposite of yielding is being unyielding: unwilling to seek a compromise or to bend in any direction. Happy couples bend. Unhappy couples stiffen and eventually break.

Are You a Bender or a Breaker?

Take the following quiz to see where you stand. All questions relate to how you and your spouse interact. Decide whether the statement is true most of the time or false most of the time.

1. If I'm right about something I probably won't back down.
   Mostly True _____ *Mostly False* _____

2. My spouse usually has good opinions.
   Mostly True _____ *Mostly False* _____

3. I get annoyed when my spouse refuses to see things my way.
   Mostly True _____ *Mostly False* _____

4. Getting along is more important than being right.
   Mostly True _____ *Mostly False* _____

5. If I keep at it I can usually get my way.
   Mostly True _____ *Mostly False* _____

6. I generally trust my spouse's judgment.
   Mostly True _____ *Mostly False* _____

7. It's hard to show patience when my spouse says things I disagree with.
   Mostly True _____ *Mostly False* _____

8. We show respect even when we disagree.
   Mostly True _____ *Mostly False* _____

9. If I don't get my way I feel owed.
    Mostly True _____ *Mostly False* _____

10. We can still see some merit to each other's views even
    when we disagree.
    Mostly True _____ *Mostly False* _____

You will have a happier relationship to the extent you
answered "Mostly True" to the even-numbered items and
"Mostly False" to the odd-numbered items. If you answered
that way eight or more times you're likely to maintain a happy
relationship. Anything less, and your relationship is at risk.

The Power of Yielding

Yielding has to be a two-way street. If only one of you yields
and the other always gets his or her way, happiness will be
stifled. Research shows that women are much more willing to
yield than men. Consequently a husband's willingness to have
a give-and-take attitude and yield to his wife's wishes much
of the time is highly predictive of a happy relationship. It's
essential therefore that men not interpret yielding as a sign of
weakness. Yielding is really an effort to be cooperative and to
find something of merit in the spouse's view. It often involves
compromising. It is an outgrowth of having respect toward
one's spouse, not disrespect toward oneself.

Had Carol and Todd been able to yield, their disagreement about whether to use software to block porn sites might

have had a different outcome. Carol would have shown that she understood Todd's need to have access to certain Web sites for his job. And Todd would have indicated that Carol was not wrong to worry about their son Brett accidentally stumbling onto a pornographic Web site. Whatever they finally chose to do would have been less important than how they arrived at that agreement. In the typical problematic marriage, it isn't the big things that a partner can be unyielding about. Often it's the small things. One partner makes a mild complaint ("We don't go out and have much fun anymore") and the other is immediately defensive and uncooperative. This causes the disagreement to escalate into an argument and finally come to a miserable end, with either no resolution or one partner throwing up his hands with a "Fine, have it your way!" attitude. A little bending and understanding would have made a huge difference.

Sometimes yielding *must* be all the way. In other words, it's good to occasionally put aside your wants and needs completely if they conflict with your partner's wants and needs. That's called *making a sacrifice* and it's good for a relationship. If you sacrifice but deeply resent it, the sacrifice won't be helpful.

? Did You Know?

Couples who are happy together share power fairly equally in the relationship. When power is one-sided, one partner possesses **overt** power but the other partner tries to balance the scales by developing **covert** power. Covert power involves passive-aggressive ways to "stick it" to one's mate, such as forgetfulness, procrastination, and manipulation. The result is a marriage that is rarely satisfying and often contentious. The key to success is shared power, sensitivity to one another's needs, and a willingness to bend.

You must find a way to see the value in letting your spouse have her way and try to find some degree of joy in it.

Compromising Isn't *Always* the Answer

Rich wanted to go to the movies with Diane. All day he imagined his arm around her, the smell of popcorn, maybe a drink afterward. Then he remembered: Tonight was her karate class. Frustrated, he thought of renting a DVD instead. It wouldn't be as much fun, but they could watch it when she returned from her class, he decided.

When Diane came home after her class and nonchalantly said she was too tired to watch the movie, Rich got mad, and she couldn't understand what all the hubbub was about.

A marriage high on compromise is a marriage low in conflict. Right? Not necessarily. Rich compromised by renting a movie instead of asking Diane to skip her karate class. Did it help? No. He resented it when she was too tired to watch it with him. That is one difficulty with compromises: compromising can sometimes make you feel as if your partner owes you something, and you resent it if you don't get your due.

Too often what appears to be a stubborn, uncompromising mate is really a frustrated partner who has compromised too much in the past—often unwittingly. How many times have you settled for something—a trip to your in-laws, a different television program, pizza instead of sushi—but never bothered to inform your partner of your kindness in compromising? Couples do that frequently. It's nice, and it's one part of the give-and-take of marriage. But if you've made too many "hidden" compromises, and now feel a bit resentful or unappreciated, you may flatly refuse to budge on some new issue. What now appears to be stubbornness and selfishness grew out of your flexibility and selflessness.

One researcher, Dr. John Gottman, studied the same couples over three years. The marriages that were happiest *in the short run* had wives who compromised a great deal. But over three years, those same marriages sharply *deteriorated* in satisfaction. Taking an uncompromising stand once in a while helped inoculate marriages against future distress.

When should you not compromise? Don't compromise your values or your health. Don't compromise if you know you'll deeply resent it later or you'll feel owed. It's best to compromise with the attitude that your sacrifice is a gift for the relationship. You may lose out in the short run—but only in the short run.

What to Do

☑ *When you disagree on what to do, focus more on what the concerns are behind your partner's viewpoint.* It's possible to care about and even agree with the underlying concerns of your partner but disagree on the way to address those concerns. For example, if one of you wanted to save a certain amount of money and one of you wanted to spend it, try to see the underlying concerns. Maybe the spender is concerned about never having much fun. Maybe the saver is worried about an upcoming bill. Try to arrive at a creative solution that meets both needs. Perhaps you will agree to not spend the money now but put aside some of it for a future bill and put aside the rest of it to spend on something more fun.

☑ *See one another as teammates, not adversaries.* When you're on the same team you want what's best for the team not just for the individuals. You realize that if a team member is selfish or inconsiderate, the team as a whole will lose.

☑ *Abandon the attitude "It's my way or no way."* That works for dictators—not married couples. Aim for a solution that addresses the concerns each of you has, not just the concerns that one of you has.

☑ *If you can't agree and all else fails, flip a coin.* It will at least ensure fairness. But the loser must not hold a grudge. The problem is not that you lost but that the two of you haven't yet found a way to cooperate or yield in a fair manner. Until that happens, you'll either argue a great deal or flip a lot of coins.

☑ *Cut back on "hidden compromises."* The more open you are about some of your thoughtful compromises, the more likely your spouse will be to show appreciation (and the less likely you'll be resentful). Understand that hidden compromises often involve *mind reading*—believing you know what your mate is thinking and feeling without asking. Reduce mind reading and you automatically reduce the number of hidden compromises. The next time you talk yourself out of going to the opera because you "know" your mate won't want to go, try telling her, "I wasn't going to ask you to attend the opera with me because you don't usually like the opera. But I thought I'd ask you anyway. Would you like to go this time?"

☑ *If you won't compromise on an issue, be sure to show compassion.* Saying, "I know it's a real sacrifice for you, but it's very important to do it my way this time" shows understanding and sensitivity for your mate. When your partner agrees to do things your way, say "Thank you" and mean it.

Keep in Mind

♡ Men especially need to find merit in their wives' viewpoints and seek solutions to differences that feel fair to both parties.

♡ You must value getting along more than you value getting your way.

♡ If you vehemently disagree with your spouse about a course of action, you are either holding on to old resentments or there is something about your partner's viewpoint that you do not understand.

♡ The benefits of compromising evaporate if you resent it later. Better to discuss your potential resentment beforehand.

♡ A noncompromising stand may be a cover for old, unsettled hurts (such as feeling unappreciated). Always compromising may mask your fear of rocking the boat.

Secret #6

Encourage Each Other's Dreams

The graduation ceremony finally ended. Hordes of twenty-two-year-olds in caps and gowns hooted and hollered, while the family and friends from the bleacher seats cascaded into the throng. And somewhere in the mass of people, Lisa, thirty-eight and a mother of three, held her cap tightly to her head while she searched for her husband Art.

"Congratulations, graduate!" said a familiar voice. Lisa turned around to see Art, all smiles and holding a single yellow rose. She hugged him tightly, grateful for the husband who encouraged her every step of the way, even when he had to take a back seat to her studies.

Your mate probably has personal dreams of glory or accomplishment—some realistic, some pie-in-the-sky. Maybe she'd like to start her own business or learn to fly an airplane, maybe he'd like to buy a parcel of land and build your vacation cottage with his own hands. Maybe you'd like to join the community theater or run for a local office, run in a marathon, do regular volunteer work for a charity organization, write a children's book, learn to ride a horse, or create a country garden second to none.

Dreams don't have to be fanciful to be meaningful. Joe's fantasy was to buy a canoe and take his wife to the nearby lake every weekend. Carol wanted to practice something she hadn't done in thirty years: ice skating. What's your dream?

Seldom Is Heard a Discouraging Word

Some spouses openly discourage a mate's ideas because they view the ideas as impractical. ("We can't afford it. And what do you know about chicken farming, anyway?") But such comments often have the reverse effect. Challenging your mate often prompts him to come up with reasons why the idea *can* work. More importantly, if your spouse regards you as unsupportive, he'll distance himself from you emotionally and probably spend more time fantasizing about his dream.

? Did You Know?

Women are much more likely than men to give up on personal dreams that do not involve the relationship. While such a thing might be called self-sacrificing, it is often done as an outgrowth of training and subtle societal pressures not to be "selfish." Husbands need to be aware of this and encourage wives to seek some kind of dream or fulfillment even if it takes time from home or the relationship. Sometimes, men will act supportive and tell their wives they should feel free to honor their dreams. But when the time comes for the women to act on those dreams, the men might be inclined to pull back their support (by refusing to alter their work hours or stay home more with the kids or give up some of their hobbies). Honoring each other's dreams is a wonderful way to say, "I love you."

Discouragement is often a clue that the idea is scary, not necessarily impractical. Your partner might be scared because your dreams clash with his expectations of your life together. Some spouses secretly feel threatened by a mate's fanciful wishes. Her dream or challenging goal suggests to you that your mate *needs more from her life than she's currently getting*—something you translate as "I'm not good enough for her."

People fantasize more than they act on their fantasies. Most of the time your spouse just wants to dream aloud, not engage in a serious discussion of the idea. Encouraging your partner's ideas, or simply agreeing, "Yeah, that sounds exciting," does no harm and builds closeness. Whether or not dreams get acted upon is less important than how close you feel to one another at the time.

One troublesome phenomenon occurs when one spouse believes the other is holding him back from achieving his dreams. Hank wanted to start his own auto-mechanic business. In truth, he had many misgivings about the idea and wasn't sure he'd attempt it even if given the opportunity. But when his wife Jane pointed out some concerns of her own, he got angry. He abandoned his dream but blamed Jane for it. If she could only be supportive, he thought, his dream would come true. Actually, Jane wasn't holding Hank back; Hank was. He was afraid to try for fear he'd fail, but rather than admit that, he conveniently blamed Jane. This is another good reason to be supportive of your mate's dreams: If they don't materialize, you won't be blamed.

Remember when you were dating? Each of you probably spoke of many dreams you had for the future. One main reason you kept on dating was that your partner didn't discourage your dreams. He listened intently and enthusiastically. You felt free to relax and be yourself with him. Just because you're married doesn't mean you stop dreaming. And *because* you are married is one good reason to care about your spouse's goals and dreams. That's what friends are for.

The Hidden Dreams Inside Your Conflicts

Dr. John Gottman at the University of Washington suggests a brilliant idea for couples when they don't think they can yield on a given position. He calls it finding the "dream within the conflict." If you have a strong opinion about something that you can't budge on, there is probably a story behind that opinion. Within that story is a dream or a wish. For example, Andy hated it when he'd arrive home to a messy house. He wasn't a fanatic and he understood that his wife, Kathy, worked, too, and that housework wasn't always her priority. Still, she had more hours at home than he did and he believed she was much too indifferent about housework than he would like. Much of the time he cleaned up areas of the house when he arrived home, thinking that it should have been cleaned before he got there. Was there a story behind his view? Yes. Listen to Andy:

> When I was a child my mother always kept the house pretty clean. After dinner the dishes were all put away, the countertops and dining room table were cleared and it just made for a very relaxing, peaceful home life. Now, when I arrive home late some nights and the dinner dishes are still unwashed and the table is cluttered with books and piles of unsorted mail, I feel like the house isn't peaceful. I can't relax. I wish I could but I can't. So I'd like more help from Kathy in that area.

Upon hearing his story, Kathy didn't automatically comply with his wishes—she thought he underestimated how much work she had to do just taking care of the kids—but she realized that Andy wasn't simply being picky and hard to satisfy. She felt some compassion for his dreams of a peaceful household. That compassion softened her stance a little and she was willing to make more of a sacrifice for him. Andy agreed to do less complaining when the house was cluttered.

Try it yourself. Think of an issue that you and your mate are at odds over. Now think of a story from your life that speaks of that issue. What early events happened that might have caused you to feel so strongly about the current issue? What hurts or losses did you suffer that led you to take an uncompromising stance now? Now tell your spouse those stories and identify what your dream or wish might be as a result of those stories. The purpose is not to cajole your spouse to do things your way. The purpose is to help each of you realize that part of the reason you're being stubborn or uncompromising is because you have an underlying dream or wish that isn't being realized. Such an understanding might help each of you soften your positions and find a compromise.

What to Do

☑ *Play a game of "Wouldn't it be great if . . ." the next time you have an opportunity to chat.* Initiate the discussion so your mate knows you're interested in her fantasies. Be as encouraging as possible. Even if you don't like your spouse's ideas, get her to elaborate by asking "And then what would you do?"

☑ *If you must express a discouraging word, do so only after your part-ner has expressed his ideas as fully as possible.* Don't immediately point out the faults of your mate's dream—that appears critical and unfeeling. Instead, talk about how the idea worries, scares, or concerns you. Saying "It worries me that you'll have less time with the family if you start this project" doesn't imply the project is a bad idea.

☑ *Applaud your mate's accomplishments, even if you wish he were doing something else.* If his role in the community play takes time from his being able to mow the lawn, mow it for him (or hire someone) with no complaints. Is your wife taking a college course, and for the past three months spent more time studying than talking to you? Help type her term paper and congratulate her on her B+. If your spouse is already involved in some project and there is no turning back, periodic complaints and verbal jabs are poisonous. If you are feeling frustrated or overwhelmed by your partner's project, report those feelings without acting on them. Saying, "I know you have to rehearse your lines for the play today, but this is one of those times I'm feeling over-whelmed" may bring you the support you desire. Complaining, "Why won't you do what I want for a change?" won't.

☑ *If you resent your partner's dream-building activities, you feel owed.* What do you think your partner owes you? A simple "thank-you"? A day off occasionally where the two of you together—or you alone—can enjoy some free time? Willing-ness to support you in *your* dream? Resentment can eat away at the foundation of your relationship. Clear the air, but don't be accusatory and hostile. Say, "I thought I could deal with this project of yours, but I'm finding it more difficult than I expected. I have some ideas on what could help."

☑ *Make a list of three strong opinions you hold and that you have a hard time yielding on.* Then write the background story that forms the basis of why you feel the way you do. Once you've written the story, share it with your partner. See if that can soften your viewpoints just enough to allow for some type of compromise or cooperative solution.

Keep in Mind

♡ It's easy to be excited for your mate when her project excites you, too. Most often, however, you need to be excited *because your mate is excited,* even if the idea doesn't thrill you.

♡ Reflexively pointing out the flaws in your mate's dream can reflect a parental "I know better" attitude. Your mate wants a partner, not a parent.

♡ A supportive spouse is not necessarily one who agrees fully with your goals. In fact, a spouse who doesn't step in your way despite misgivings may be the most supportive of all.

♡ One thing is for sure: Whether you support or impede your spouse in her dreams, she'll never forget.

Recognize Your Role in a Problem

"My wife Amy doesn't want to have sex," Alan said. "That's the problem. Oh, we'll have it once in a while, but it's always my idea and it's never frequent enough. What's wrong with her?"

After a full assessment of the problem, a major stumbling block to Alan and his wife having a satisfying sex life was revealed. Early on, Alan hadn't distinguished between the times when Amy wanted to make love and when she wanted only affection. Amy never spoke up about it, either. Consequently, she began making excuses to avoid sex, believing that Alan was "only after one thing." Her distancing just increased his desires and made it more likely that the next time they were affectionate he'd push for something more. Neither one recognized they were caught in a vicious cycle, a "marriage-go-round." The more he pursued, the more she distanced. The more she distanced, the more he pursued. Until they halted that cycle, their sexual relationship was destined to create misery.

Melissa and Mike had a different problem but a similar vicious-cycle pattern. When Mike disciplined his stepson, Danny, Melissa often felt Mike was too strict. Concerned about her son's adjustment to his new "father," Melissa often compensated for Mike's strictness by being lenient. When Mike > > >

>>> observed Melissa being lenient, he viewed it as undermining his position as a parent. Hurt and angry, he'd be lenient with Danny until he couldn't bear it, then would clamp down somewhat harshly. Melissa would complain again of his strictness, and the cycle repeated itself.

Marriage-Go-Rounds: When Solutions Become Part of the Problem

Marital dissatisfactions persist because of problems *and* because of the ways couples try to resolve their problems. Alan believed the "problem" was Amy's avoidance of sex. But his solution (to show patience for a while then push more strongly for sex) made the problem worse. Melissa thought the "problem" was Mike's strictness. But her solution (complaining to Mike and showing more lenience toward her son) aggravated the situation.

Melissa's and Alan's solutions did make a kind of sense. In some other context they might have worked. Ironically, it is precisely because those solutions made sense that Melissa and Alan didn't consider abandoning them when the desired effects weren't forthcoming. Instead, they intensified their efforts (much like pressing harder on the accelerator when your car is stuck in the mud) and unwittingly aggravated the situation.

Common examples where the cure prolongs the disease:

- A husband dislikes disclosing his feelings and prefers "reason" to emotion. That frustrates his wife, who becomes emotional. Her emotionality alarms him and prompts him to reason with her while keeping his feelings to himself.

● A wife who thinks her husband is "hiding something" interrogates him and scrutinizes his behavior. He resents the scrutiny and becomes less talkative and more evasive, reinforcing her belief that he is hiding something from her.

● A husband, uncomfortable with conflict, avoids discussing an obvious marital problem with his wife, who is angered and hurt by his withdrawal. The tension between them mounts, and the husband withdraws further.

While it's common to lay most of the blame for a marital problem at your partner's feet, the truth is that many marital conflicts are *reciprocal* in nature. That is, each of you acts and responds toward the other in a manner that perpetuates dissatisfaction. One way to tell whether you and your mate are trapped on a marriage-go-round is first to determine whether you have any opposing traits. Is one of you responsible with money, while the other is irresponsible? Assertive/unassertive? Boring/the life of the party? Tidy/sloppy? Outgoing/shy? Spontaneous/planner? Do you devote time and energy trying to convert your spouse? If so, you are probably reinforcing, to some extent, the exact behaviors you want changed. That doesn't mean that each of you is equally responsible for the current problem. It might be that one of you is much more unreasonable, uncooperative, or difficult. For the problem to improve, that person will probably have to do more of the changing. Still, while you may or may not have created a problem with your partner, you are probably helping to unwittingly keep it going. Another way to discern if you and your partner are trapped is to recognize that you keep arguing repeatedly over the same issues to no avail. If you keep doing what you've been doing, nothing will change.

Reduce Defensiveness

When defensiveness is strong, a partner denies any degree of responsibility for a problem or responds to a complaint with the attitude, "Me? What about *you?*" Defensive people view themselves as innocent victims. A problem is someone else's fault. A defensive stance usually makes the other partner more annoyed and aggressive so the complaint escalates into an argument.

While it's true that some people get defensive very easily, the level of defensiveness usually corresponds to the level of perceived attack. A complaint (not a personal attack) often results in little or no defensiveness. But harsh criticisms (where one person is attacked as being defective in some way) almost always create defensiveness. If a couple has a history of making personal attacks against one another then even a minor complaint might be taken as a personal insult. To reduce defensiveness, each partner must be willing to identify and admit to a role in any problem. To do that, neither partner should be attacked. One or more of the following usually characterizes attacks:

- A harsh tone.
- A sneer or some other nonverbal gesture that suggests contempt or disgust.

- Criticisms not about someone's actions but about one's character or personality (for example, "You're a liar . . . You don't care . . . You're lazy . . . ").
- Use of all-inclusive words and phrases such as "You always . . . You never . . . Every time . . . "
- Personal insults.
- Verbal or physical threats.
- A refusal to really hear the other person out.

No dialogue will ever be productive as long as any of the above occurs. Either the attacker must stop or the attackee must walk away and resume talks later when cooler heads prevail.

The Blame Game

Blaming is another vehicle for a marriage-go-round. Once a blamer labels a spouse lazy, insensitive, a sex maniac, etc., he doesn't have to consider his own role in the problem. The blamed partner then feels unjustly criticized, and the battle lines are drawn. Blamers have a tendency to withdraw in contempt precisely at the time their spouse is willing to be responsive. Consequently, partners can't seem to work on the problem at the same time. After a while, blamers see only the evidence that supports their negative beliefs about their partners, selectively ignoring evidence to the contrary.

Clearly the trick is to stop blaming one another and stop reapplying "solutions" to marital discord that don't work.

What to Do

☑ *State aloud (to yourself) your ongoing method of resolving a marital issue.* Examples, as suggested by Richard Driscoll in *The Ties That Bind*:

- "I complain to my wife that she's overweight so that she'll be motivated to exercise."
- "I avoid having sex so he'll understand how angry I am."
- "I mumble when he speaks to me so he'll give me quiet time alone."
- "I avoid telling her how I really feel because I don't want to 'rock the boat.'"

Repeat your statement out loud five times. Now answer this: Is it working? If the answer is "no," try a different "solution."

☑ *If your attempted solutions to improve marital interactions have failed and your prescription for success is to intensify your efforts, stop right there.* Daniel Wile, author of *After the Honeymoon: How Conflicts Can Improve Your Relationship,* suggests that you tell your mate exactly what you were doing, and why, and tell him you think you may have only made the problem worse. Example: "I wanted some time alone to relax after work but I knew you wanted me to talk to you about your day. So I did my usual thing of going into the den without saying a word, hoping you'd get the message. Chances are, though, I only made you feel neglected." Such remarks open the door to a constructive discussion about how to get both of your needs met. The remarks are also nonaccusatory, something your mate will appreciate.

☑ *Practice the art of relabeling.* Most behaviors can be classified as negative or positive, depending upon your mood. Is your aloof husband avoiding you or is he tired or preoccupied? Is she boring or content? Stubborn, or clear about what he wants? Overemotional or sentimental? Passive or tolerant of the way things are? Suspicious or inquisitive? Lazy or unregimented? Ask yourself whether you've ever done any of the behaviors you dislike your spouse doing. If you have, what were your reasons for acting that way? Chances are you'll see more merit in your behavior than when your partner behaves the same way. Give him the same benefit of the doubt.

☑ *Assume your partner is behaving in a way that she feels is appropriate and in everyone's best interest.* (That's probably how she feels, anyway.) Visualize her acting in the way you dislike, but also visualize yourself responding to her more kindly. Get a clear, strong image of yourself doing that. How were you able to imagine yourself responding differently? You did so by changing your thinking. Ascribing benign or positive motives to your partner's actions may help you respond more constructively.

☑ *Think twice.* If you believe you are being unfairly labeled or blamed, first acknowledge any merit to the complaints. No, you're not *always* insensitive to her feelings, but is there any merit at all in what she's saying? If so, admit it. Then you can point out where you disagree.

☑ *Predict exceptions to the rule* (as suggested in *In Search of Solutions: A New Direction in Psychotherapy*). You and your mate don't *always* act in an unproductive manner. Once in a while your "lazy" husband tidies up. Once in a while your "critical" wife is complimentary. Once in a while you and your mate have a peaceful evening despite a lousy day at the office. How come? Predict with your mate which upcoming scenarios you or he won't respond to in a problematic way, and what factors will help bring that about. Predicting exceptions to the rule makes each of you more aware of behavior patterns that once were automatic. Once aware, you are in a better position to change them.

☑ *Use numbers.* If you've expended energy trying to get your mate to change certain behaviors, first rate from 1 to 10 how invested you believe your mate is in changing (a 10 means he or she is extremely motivated to change). Then rate the degree of investment you have in your mate changing. Rule of thumb: If you are more invested in (and thus more anxious about) your mate changing than he or she is, change is less likely to occur. It would be like pulling dead weight. Better to determine what it is you hope to gain by your mate changing, and then try to get that need met (at least partially) some other way. Your mate's reluctance to change was most likely based in part on his feeling that you didn't understand his need not to change.

Backing off may help him feel more understood and can actually increase his willingness to accommodate you.

Keep in Mind

♡ It is not your partner's negative behaviors per se that cause you difficulty. It is what you think about the behaviors that lead to your feeling troubled.

♡ If a solution didn't work despite an honest effort, "more of the same" won't work.

♡ Once you recognize your role in the continuation of a problem, you have something worthwhile to change.

♡ Partners locked in an ongoing struggle that's going nowhere have important things to say that they don't believe have been fully heard or understood.

♡ You are always at a disadvantage when you are more invested in someone changing than he is.

Secret #8

Love It Up with Sex and Affection

Want a sex life to match that of the happiest couples? Jumping into bed together more often just won't suffice.

While it's true that happily married partners are very satisfied with their sexual relationship, it's not because they have sex more often. According to Andrew Greeley in *Faithful Attraction: Discovering Intimacy, Love, and Fidelity in American Marriages*, sexual experimentation is more important to happy couples than frequency of sex. But the most important source of marital happiness has to do with the character of one's spouse. According to a major national survey, a spouse who makes you feel important, who is kind, gentle, exciting, and good with children—*and* who is sexually satisfying and prone to sexual experimentation—most powerfully influences your marital satisfaction.

So how do you best add zest to your love life? First, enhance your appeal as a spouse by having more intimate conversations and by showing more consideration and nonsexual affection. *Then* add some novelty and creativity to your lovemaking (use body oils, erotic play, try different positions—anything out of the ordinary will do). It's a formula that works.

Mismatched Sexual Desire

Husbands often underestimate the amount of interest their wives have in sex. Almost 100 percent of romance novels are read by women. (Most romance novels contain highly erotic passages.) Greeley reports that women fantasize about sex as intensely as men, though less frequently. In fact, for women over forty, engaging in acts of "sexual abandon" with their mate makes them feel more attractive and appealing. By being more communicative, considerate, and affectionate, husbands can tap into the sexual energy their wives already possess.

Also uncommon is for wives to understand what the act of making love means to their husbands. To believe that their husbands are only after one thing misses something fundamental. Men may know they are loved by their wives, but they *feel* loved when they make love. Husbands who complain they aren't getting enough sex may be feeling they aren't getting enough love.

Mismatched sexual desire is found in almost every couple. One partner usually prefers having sex a bit more often than the other. But even if a couple was perfectly matched in their level of sexual desire (say, wanting sex twice a week) you can bet they would, from time to time, disagree on what days of any particular week (or time of day) they should have sex. If the differences in sexual desire are mishandled, the gap between their levels of desire will widen.

Managing Your Differences in Sexual Desire

The differences a couple has about sexual desire start to become a problem when one partner feels the other is being inconsiderate or that the other partner's preferences are a form of rejection. So if the husband is dissatisfied because they are having sex less frequently than he'd like, he might regard his wife's "Not tonight, dear" as a form of rejection. If he gets irritable or pushy, she then might regard him as being insensitive or selfish. Once partners have labeled each other in those ways, they tend to dig in and get stubborn. They each feel unfairly treated. This pattern only gets worse if one partner grudgingly "gives in" to the other. If the one partner grudgingly goes along with sex, he or she will then pull away afterward and feel entitled to be left alone. If the other partner gives in and stops pursuing sex, he or she will eventually think, "I've waited long enough" and resume pushing for sex. The struggle will continue with each side believing "If you loved me, you'd have sex on my terms," which is an irrational and unfair attitude.

In marriages where each partner's level of sexual desire is not affected by past sexual trauma and is simply a personal preference, there are three things a couple can do to manage their differences in sexual desire. This will help to either shorten the gap or make differences tolerable:

- Increase consideration and thoughtfulness in all areas of the relationship.
- Increase affection, especially nonsexual affection.
- Learn to accept your differences without resentment.

Increase Overall Thoughtfulness

Please read **Secret #3** Magical Attentiveness for a more detailed exploration of this topic. It's important to understand that in any loving and caring relationship, the sexual aspect of the relationship is intertwined with the broader category of how well you generally "get along." Considerate and thoughtful acts go a long way to increasing sexual appetites. Despite the fact that most mothers are now part of the outside work force and that men are more involved in housekeeping and child-rearing than ever before, women still do more of it. When a man does his fair share of the home-related work and child-rearing, it really is a form of foreplay to an overworked, harried mother. It's not an overstatement to say that in order to have great sex on Friday night, for a woman foreplay starts on Wednesday in the form of helpful gestures.

It gets complicated when the frequency of sex is too low and the frustrated partner cuts back on thoughtful and caring gestures as a way to show displeasure. Now the other partner feels less cared about, and sexual desire will diminish even further. If you are frustrated by a reduction in sexual intimacy, ask about it in a gentle, nonaccusatory way. "I've noticed we don't make love as often as I'd like. I miss it. Is there anything I can do to help you get in the mood?" Such a remark is not a guarantee of success but it's much better than pouting or pulling away from your partner or being demanding and accusatory.

Increase Nonsexual Affection

It's all in your perception. If your partner hugs you and then starts pawing at you, do you take that as a sign that he finds you appealing or do you take it as a sign that he wants sex? And if you take it as a sign that he wants sex, do you see that as a good thing or an indication that he's basically an animal and only cares about you for sexual release? Sexual affection is a very good thing in a marriage. It is playful and a sign that your mate finds you attractive and appealing. But too often sexual affection is the only type of affection you get that lasts longer than two seconds. When that happens routinely, you can lose your sense of feeling cared about and feel instead like a sexual object. And when that happens you will find yourself pulling away not only from sexual affection, but also from affection in general. That will cause a ripple effect. The more you pull away, the less sexual you will be. The less sexual you are, the more your spouse will pursue sex or attempt to show sexual affection as a means to get sex. You will pull away even more and the push-pull pattern will continue and eventually result in an overall detachment.

Assuming no health problems exist and the marriage is at least somewhat satisfying, an increase in nonsexual affection will over time improve the quality of your togetherness and therefore increase the likelihood of more frequent and satisfying sex.

An affectionate spouse tells you that you are loved and desired despite a sagging body or cranky disposition. Showing affection is a way of caring, of soothing the bumps and bruises of everyday life. Everybody needs a hug.

Learn to Accept Your Differences

You probably entered your relationship with differences, large or small, in sexual desire. But if you mishandled the way you coped with those differences you unwittingly widened the gap. By improving thoughtfulness and nonsexual affection you can lessen the gap. But a gap may still exist regardless of what you do to be a great spouse. When that happens you must learn to emotionally accept the differences in sexual desire. To accept doesn't mean you like the situation or find it appealing; it means you will no longer emotionally oppose the situation. To accept doesn't mean you can never speak up about your preferences or that you must always give in to your partner. Imagine a couple where the man prefers sex about twice a week and the woman prefers having sex about twice a month. That's a fourfold difference in desire. For the man to accept the woman's preference doesn't mean he can't push for sex more often once in a while. It does mean he won't rail against her if it doesn't happen. But for the woman in this case to accept her man's sexual desires, she needs to lean in his direction once in awhile, too. If acceptance is mutual it means there will be a give and a take.

? Did You Know?

One of the most reliable ways to measure and monitor your marital happiness is the following (assuming good physical health): Calculate the number of times you had intercourse in a certain time frame (say, two weeks) and subtract the number of arguments you had. (An argument occurred any time one spouse became "uncooperative.") If the answer is a positive number, you're probably happy. If it's a negative number, you're probably not, according to a study conducted by John Howard and Robyn Dawes designed to predict marital happiness.

This method reflects marital happiness. It is not a formula for improving happiness. Automatically increasing the frequency of intercourse or reducing the number of arguments won't necessarily make you a happy couple. But it is a good way to monitor your progress in improving the happiness in your marriage.

What to Do

☑ *For one month, be affectionate with your mate eight to ten times a day.* It needn't be passionate. If there have been arguments lately about sex or if most of the time you tend to offer sexual affection, be sure your shows of affection are nonsexual. Caress his back as you pass by him in the kitchen. Squeeze her hand. Kiss him on the cheek. Rub her shoulder. Sexual displays of affection (such as pinching his bottom) are fine if your mate is receptive, but the goal of this exercise is to be affectionate without it necessarily leading to sex. This is especially important if one spouse has complained that the other can't be affectionate without being sexual.

☑ *Set a loving mood early in the day.* Give "Good morning" and "Good night" kisses whenever possible. Show tenderness. Smile warmly at your spouse. Cuddle in bed for a few extra minutes. Don't leave in the morning without a kiss or hug. Ask if there is something you can do that would make your partner's day go a little easier. Call during the day to say "Hi." If you had an argument the night before, don't spend the morning sulking or complaining. If the argument can't be settled before work, say you'll settle it that night and do your best to be pleasant. You can be angry at each other and still be pleasant.

☑ *Once in a while, schedule lovemaking at least twelve hours ahead of time.* That gives each of you time to gear up, fantasize about it, and accomplish all the minor tasks that might ordinarily intrude on your time together. A nice touch: Call your mate or leave a short note expressing some sexual fantasy you have about the upcoming event. For your next two lovemaking sessions, plan to not reach orgasm—both of you. You can come close to orgasm if you'd like, but stop short of that final pleasure. Without that common goal in mind, you and your mate will have lingering foreplay and sensual body caresses. You'll delight in sensations you ordinarily ignore. You'll likely learn something new about what pleases your partner. And when you finally do reach orgasm later, it will knock your socks off (if they're not already off).

☑ *To improve desire, think of a time when you were head-over-heels attracted to your mate.* Visualize the scene fully. What essential qualities from that scene does your mate still possess? A certain look, a smile, a way of speaking, a way of touching? Sometimes, a little preparation (by way of fantasy) can improve your desire for, and enjoyment of, sex.

☑ If *sex has become a bit stale and predictable, agree with your mate to have more spontaneous sex.* By definition, spontaneous sex is unplanned and occurs at a time or place not usually set aside for making love. Take turns initiating it. When your mate is the initiator, then you have the privilege of deciding where, how, and how long you'll make love together.

☑ *To increase intimacy (and possibly sexual desire) read a novel to your partner.* It helps make an isolated act (reading) an intimate one, and can add to your excitement if there are any erotic passages in the book.

☑ *Care about your appearance and your health.* Very few of us have the shape and stamina of Olympic athletes, but all of us can try to look and dress in a manner that appeals to our mate. Plump or scrawny, the right outfit, cologne, or hairstyle can really please a partner. And there is nothing like knowing you are attractive to your mate to make you feel good about yourself and more sexually alive.

Keep in Mind

♡ In general, the best way to increase the frequency of sex is to dramatically increase the frequency of sincere, non-sexual affection.

♡ Sincere, open revelation of feelings is the most intimate thing you can do.

♡ There is a tendency for men in their middle-adult years to be more sensual (as opposed to genital) in their sexual approach. That usually makes for better sex.

♡ It's okay not to feel like having sex, but never withhold sex as a punishment.

♡ If your partner is going through a sexually quiet period, making demands won't help. Remain physically affectionate and emotionally in touch with your partner, and neither you nor your mate will feel rejected or misunderstood.

Secret #9

Take Time for Yourself

"What are we having for supper tonight?"
"Where are we going this weekend?"
"When can we spend more time together."
"When should we visit your parents?"
"What should we say to Jeffrey about his report card?"

We, we, we. Being married certainly is a "we" proposition. And when kids enter the picture, whatever sense of privacy or self you enjoyed goes down the drain faster than Winnie the Pooh soap suds. But remaining happily married requires an "I" focus, too.

Is taking time for yourself a selfish preoccupation? It can be if you routinely neglect the needs of others. But one of the more selfish things you can do is to neglect yourself. When you neglect yourself you eventually become needy. You then require more help from others and resent it when help isn't forthcoming. Selfishness can unravel a relationship. But so can an *absence* of selfishness.

Who were you before you became a "we"? Does any part of that person still exist? When you're alone, who is the "me" inside of you? Do you ever have quiet time to be alone?

Renew Yourself

People stop dreaming when they think it's time to wake up. Mortgages, taxes, career ladders, children, aches and pains, hair loss, a fondness for quieter music—are all reminders that you're older now and that the real world must be faced, not an imaginary one. But if facing the real world means abandoning personal dreams or losing your sense of individuality, you may feel imprisoned by your commitments and smothered by your intimate relationships.

Happy couples not only balance time together with time apart, they use their individual time to replenish themselves. Self-renewal is more than collapsing into your favorite chair to watch sitcoms on television. Without self-renewal, a spouse often believes his partner should fill the void in his life. When that partner inevitably fails in filling the void, the spouse disengages somewhat from the marriage, knowing "something is missing" but falsely assuming that the "something" is marriage-related, rather than self-related.

The first kind of self-renewal involves taking time to do more of the things you really enjoy. Vacations sometimes serve that purpose, though most people could use more than the allotted two weeks. Learning to relax, to enjoy solitude, to gaze at a night sky and feel a stirring of wonder and peace—all help you to reorient yourself to your neglected inner world.

A second level of self-renewal is more profound and longer lasting. It involves having a vision, a mission, or a purpose for your life. Too many people with worthwhile goals talk themselves out of even trying. They convince themselves that they already have too many responsibilities. Besides, dreams are risky. But meaningful dreams won't ever go completely away because they represent what you want your life to count for. Will your dream still be important a year, or five years, from now? When your life is nearing its end, will you regret your decision to forsake that dream? If you answered, "Yes," you have a dream worth pursuing.

Henry's dream was to entertain. He was married with two kids and had a secure job as a computer programmer, but he also sang well and played a mean piano. He never followed his dream, and blamed his wife. True, she didn't like the idea that as an entertainer he'd spend his weekends in clubs rather than at home. But he never took the time to tell her how

❓ Did You Know?

If your dream involves a new career path or any direction that will increase stress in your life, make sure you find time to connect with your spouse in meaningful ways. Studies show that couples under stress that develop the values of the "masculine role" (reduced affection; restricted emotions; preoccupation with success) grew more dissatisfied with each other and their lives. Building a dream is wonderful but don't tear down the dream of a wonderful marriage and home life in the process. Find ways to build your dream (or encourage your partner's dream) while remaining lovingly connected to your spouse.

important his dream was to him. He never bothered to listen to her concerns with compassion and without complaint. He never tried to negotiate with her in a way that might meet both their needs. His dream was his responsibility, but he never understood that.

Sometimes a person lets go of a dream to commit more strongly to the marriage dream (for example, by turning down a promotion that would have required spending too much time away from home). A sacrifice, to be sure, but done for a worthwhile reason—to allow the marriage to flourish. It's not always easy to know which dream should be followed and which should fade. But happy couples keep dreams alive.

Have you given up a bit of yourself over the years? Do you always think in terms of "we" or "us" and rarely "I"? If so, you're preventing your spouse from enjoying a major source of marital pleasure: a partner who likes himself, enjoys himself, and who has personal goals and ambitions.

What to Do

☑ *Respond to this statement:* "If I had complete freedom (more opportunity, more money, support from my spouse, etc.), I'd probably devote more time to _____." If you come up with an answer that you can't shake off, you owe it to yourself to take the idea seriously.

☑ *Make a list of twenty activities you'd enjoy doing by yourself over the next several months:* taking in a few matinees, exercising, reading more spy novels, taking nature photos, going to a bar with friends, canoeing, fishing, taking a class on flower arranging, getting a babysitter for an afternoon while you go to a museum. Now start doing some of them! At a minimum try two per month. To improve your motivation, keep the list posted in a prominent place. Every time you do an activity, place a check mark next to that item on your list. Ask your mate to encourage you. If one of the items listed is extremely special but too difficult or expensive to do regularly (taking a weekend trip, attending a Broadway play, dining at a posh restaurant, etc.), use that as a reward for accomplishing a specific number of the smaller activities.

☑ *For three days, note* all *of your activities and how much time you devoted to each.* Finding time for self-renewal often requires curtailing other activities. Can you eliminate a half-hour of television daily? For a few months can you get in the habit of tidying up the children's toys only once a day (perhaps just before bedtime) instead of doing it as often as you ordinarily do? Can you make creative use of your lunch hour? (Picnic in the park, exercise, listen to music from a portable CD player, etc.?) Prioritize. Are you spending too much time on less satisfying activities? If so, can you rearrange priorities, even for just a few weeks?

☑ *Build a dream.* Devote at least fifteen minutes a day, four days a week, for one month to quiet introspection. Relaxing background music might add to the atmosphere. Contemplate a dream for your future. You'll know you've hit pay dirt when the vision excites you, gives you a burst of energy, and stays with you when your fifteen minutes are over. Once the dream is clear, what is the first step you could take to help make that dream an eventual reality? What would be the second step? Obviously, you don't have to act on your dream immediately, but focusing on the necessary and challenging steps required to make your dream a reality can boost your motivation.

Keep in Mind

♡ Whether you abandon a dream or "go for it," the responsibility for the decision is totally yours.

♡ Taking time to renew yourself can be one of the nicest things you do for your partner, too.

♡ The failure to be selfish once in a while can render you needy, helpless, or demanding—which will only make you more selfish.

♡ Women, more than men, are willing to abandon personal dreams for relationship dreams. Is that always wise? Can't you do both?

Secret #10

Be Positively Optimistic

You don't need a major calamity in your life to become depressed. In one study published in the *Journal of Behavioral Medicine,* daily hassles (minor arguments, broken machinery, traffic tie-ups, etc.) predicted depression better than did major life events (serious illness, death of loved one, etc.). And if your marriage is not satisfying, chances are that the ordinary day-to-day hassles will be even more upsetting. Why? Because unhappy, pessimistic thoughts breed more unhappy thoughts. When you are happy and all is well in your life, a fender-bender or an insensitive remark from your spouse can be shrugged off. But when you are unhappy, such events make you feel frustrated and less in charge of your life, which can cultivate a "Why is everyone against me?" attitude. Pessimism has a way of clouding over all aspects of your life, not just the troubling parts. Men and women in unhappy marriages can become pessimistic. That is one reason why they are twenty-five times more likely to become clinically depressed than couples in a satisfying marriage.

You Gotta Have Hope!

Successful couples are, by and large, hopeful and optimistic couples. Optimists are healthier and happier and they live longer than pessimists. They are more creative, better problem solvers, and more friendly and helpful. When adversity strikes, optimists are more likely to persevere, to accept life's challenges, to cope well, and to collect fewer scars. Pessimists are likely to give up sooner, especially when the going gets tough. And pessimists are more likely to become depressed during trying times. Compare the following pessimistic/optimistic comments. See for yourself how one's attitude can generate either happiness or misery:

Optimistic: "Even if we disagree, I know my wife will eventually understand how I feel, and I'll understand her."
Pessimistic: "My wife never understands me."

Optimistic: "This hasn't been an easy time for us but we're confident we'll get through it. We'll find a way."
Pessimistic: "We've tried to work things out. It's hopeless."

Optimistic: "We'll just keep trying until we succeed."
Pessimistic: "Things improved for a while until my husband went back to his old ways. Why bother trying again?"

Each of the optimistic examples reflects one of the three underpinnings to hope. First, hope takes root when you feel *understood.* Knowing that your thoughts and feelings make sense—that you are not crazy or foolish—gives you reason to believe that answers to your concerns exist and may be forthcoming. Believing that your spouse understands you (versus his insisting "You shouldn't feel that way!") enhances togetherness and can protect you from despair. Unhappy couples often feel misunderstood by their mates, which diminishes their hope that they can resolve differences.

? Did You Know?

You can dispute your negative, pessimistic thinking using the mnemonic A-E-I-O-U:

A. *Alternative.* Look for alternative ways to interpret events. ("My husband hardly notices me when he comes home from work. Is he being inconsiderate of my needs *or is he pre-occupied with some problem?*") Come up with as many possible alternatives to negative interpretations. Don't automatically believe the worst.

E. *Evidence.* Look for evidence to the contrary. Look for facts that would point to the negative effects of whatever is bothering you as being temporary and restricted, not permanent and pervasive. Example: Change "He never appreciates what I do" to "He has appreciated me many times before."

I. *Importance and Implications.* How important is this really? Yes, a marriage is very important, but are you making the problem more dire than it is?

O. *Overblown.* Is your language overblown? Avoid catastrophic words. Is your situation truly *terrible* or is it just difficult? Avoid absolutistic words such as always or never. ("We'll always be in debt. We'll never be able to afford a house.") Ask yourself if the negative things you are telling yourself are absolutely true. Chances are they are exaggerations.

U. *Usefulness.* How useful is it to think the way you do? Does it help you make progress or does it slow you down?

Second, hope is nourished when you possess *faith*—not a blind faith that matters will work out—but a faith that resources are available to you to make success likely. When you have friends and family who care, your outlook isn't quite so bleak. And when you believe you possess the skills necessary to get you through a difficult period, it's easier to feel optimistic. Most unhappy couples don't believe they possess adequate problem-solving or communication skills, and consequently feel more hopeless.

Finally, hope requires *committed work*. The hopeful persevere despite setbacks. Unhappy couples, feeling weary, misunderstood, and short on faith, abandon efforts to improve the relationship much sooner.

No matter what your difficulty, if you can trust that someone *understands* your pain; if you can nurture the *faith* that you have the resources to cope; and if you *commit* yourself to overcoming your difficulties; hope will thrive, and so will you.

Optimism During Trying Times

When anxiety rises during a personal or family crisis, coping efforts become more rigid. Someone who likes the company of others during minor difficulties may demand *togetherness* during moments of intense stress. Alternatively, someone who prefers time alone when stressed may go into hiding when matters seem overwhelming. All the skills that couples use to keep their marriage healthy during calm times—negotiation, compromise, tolerance, understanding—are stretched to the limit during a crisis.

Pete and Patty went through hard times when he lost his job. Some days, when no job interviews were scheduled and Pete returned home from the unemployment office feeling forlorn, he just wanted to be left alone.

"How did it go?" Patty would ask.

"The same."

"Well, you should hear back from some of the other companies this week. I'm sure they were impressed with your application."

"Yeah, sure," he'd mumble, walking out of the room.

"I just wanted to know how he was doing," Pat confided to me later. "I wanted him to know I was there for him, that I don't consider him a failure, and that together we'll get through this. Why won't he let me help him?"

Many men have a harder time asking for help than do women. Sometimes they don't want to appear weak, or they don't want to add to their spouse's burdens, so they retreat into themselves. For a short-term problem, such a withdrawal probably won't have adverse effects and may help the situation if the man is able to sort things out for himself. But when problems drag on, retreating may add to the difficulties as partners feel more and more disconnected from each other.

In the above example, Patty's frustration was not just because Pete wanted to be left alone. She was frustrated because she believed it was in his best interest to talk (and she was probably right) and she felt less competent as a spouse when he didn't respond the way she wanted. A more helpful way for Patty to respond might have been, "It looks like you'd rather be alone for a while. Why don't I call you when dinner's ready? I do want to talk to you about some things, but I'm willing to wait until later."

The Plus Side of Adversity

Think for a moment of all the different friends you've had over your lifetime. Chances are, the friends you still feel closest to—even if you live 1,000 miles away and rarely see one another—are the ones who were by your side during some challenging time of your life. Trying times have a way of bonding relationships. If a couple can get through hard times with no blaming and a greater sense of connectedness, a special bond develops that time cannot weaken. Knowing that you survived a personal or family crisis can also increase your confidence in being able to cope with future adversity.

? Did You Know?

Men and women often have different approaches to grief? In a study of 127 parents whose child died from Sudden Infant Death Syndrome conducted by John DeFrain and published in the *Journal of Marriage and Family Therapy,* 85 percent of the partners did not match each other in their grief response. Most men cried less, talked less often about the death, and expressed less emotion than their wives. Yet according to the researchers, the men suffered as much as the women. They were better at hiding their suffering, however. Fathers felt a responsibility to be caretaker and a source of strength for their wives. Both parents faced the dilemma of having to grieve their loss and at the same time deal with their day-to-day responsibilities. The other children still needed attention, and somebody had to return to work sooner than desired in order to provide for the family.

Still, the couples in the study did an excellent job in helping each other cope with the loss. Those who coped best did not fall prey to strict social stereotypes. The mothers were not always over-emotional and helpless; the husbands were not always strong and silent. Each grieved, and each allowed the other to grieve without blaming, chastising, or making unreasonable demands.

Adversity also helps to make your life more meaningful. As often as not, trying times help you to reprioritize your values. You learn to appreciate the importance of your relationships. Little things you'd ordinarily overlook become precious in your eyes.

It's possible, and necessary, to hold hands with your mate during difficult times. Each of you may have your idiosyncratic ways of coping, but staying connected to your mate can be a soothing balm in an otherwise painful period. When the crisis has passed (or there is a lull), take some time for the two of you to be alone together. Go away for a weekend trip. Hire a sitter for the kids and spend the day relaxing with your mate.

What to Do

☑ *Keep a list of the specific ways you think your marriage is at least average, if not better than most.* Research shows that if you view your relationship as better than most, you'll persist when the going gets rough. You may not like your spouse's way of disciplining the children, but is she a devoted mother? A considerate person? Able to negotiate with you? Financially responsible? When problems arise, pessimists lose sight of what's strong about a relationship, which undermines their faith and hope.

☑ *If your mate is troubled by a loss or other painful situation, give her first the message "I love you," not the message "You need me."* A sense of control is important in coping. Taking complete charge or giving advice prematurely without getting a clear sense of what your mate really needs may diminish her sense of control. Accept, never challenge, a grieving partner's feelings. Don't try to talk him out of feelings just because they make you uncomfortable or you don't understand them. A spouse who feels misunderstood may turn away from you at a time when your presence can be beneficial. Listen fully and summarize what your partner tells you so that each of you can be sure it was fully understood.

☑ *Take turns.* If you and your mate have opposite ways of coping—he wants time alone, you want time together; you want to be able to talk on a moment's notice, he prefers scheduled dialogues; etc.—agree to take turns having things handled your way. Joel Bergman, in an article published in *Group and Family Therapy,* suggests one example of taking turns: on odd days of the month your spouse gets his way and on even days, you get your way. Knowing in advance that your need won't get swept aside helps build patience and tolerance of your partner's needs.

☑ *Encourage, but don't insist, that your mate "talk out" his troubling feelings.* Some people aren't comfortable expressing difficult feelings. While it is healthier for them to talk, persistent efforts to get them to talk may backfire. Some men feel they must be "the strong one" in the family. To discuss painful feelings can make them feel weak. Others fear that expressing deep feelings will cause them to lose emotional control. Some ways to help encourage a reluctant spouse to express him- or herself:

● Suggest that she write out her feelings (privately).
● Ask him to help you understand why he prefers not to discuss his feelings. Tell him you won't debate or challenge his reasons, but that you would like to better understand.

- Speculate on what you think she may be feeling. Example: "It wouldn't surprise me if you felt scared . . . "
- Comment that he must be feeling lonely.

☑ *Reassure the children.* During stressful times, young children worry, too. That may show up as temper tantrums, disobedience, school or social problems, or withdrawal. If there is something they can *reasonably* do that will ease your burdens (a few more chores, making fewer requests for new clothes or extra spending money, etc.), ask for their help and show your appreciation. Most important, spend extra quality time with them.

Keep in Mind

♡ An optimistic attitude strengthens togetherness, goodwill, and fondness.

♡ All problems are temporary. They either disappear or we figure out a way to manage them and move forward. Even if the pain doesn't completely go away, it doesn't have to get in your way.

♡ Problems don't make or break you. It's your response to a problem that is vital to your success.

♡ In trying times, your spouse is coping in the way he or she thinks is for the best. Keep that in mind if you want your mate to do something different.

Supersize Your Intimacy

Remember when you and your spouse were dating? As you started to fall in love, intimacy levels were probably very high. You thought about each other when you were apart; you had lengthy conversations where you each disclosed your hopes, fears, and dreams; you went to new places and did a lot of enjoyable things together; and you probably couldn't keep your hands off of each other. Those levels of intimacy were exotic, exuberant, delicious—and alas, over-inflated. The process of falling in love does have a biological component that sends hormones racing throughout your body and makes you say and do and think things you wouldn't otherwise say, do, or think. Falling in love is exhilarating and wonderful. Staying in love is also wonderful but less intoxicating. And therein lies the rub.

Staying in love requires regular doses of intimacy and an occasional supersized dose of it. But the average couple tends to reduce their overall levels of intimacy as time goes on. If the levels fall below a certain magical point, the marriage will get bland and possibly break apart. Sustaining higher levels of intimacy is actually fairly easy once you get into a rhythm. But it helps to understand what intimacy is really about—and it's not just about sex.

Intimate Pathways: The Four Ts

Intimacy is a deep, shared connection to another person involving some form of self-disclosure and accompanied by feelings of mutual caring. An intimate act is measured more by the quality of the relationship (the quality of caring or love) than by the act itself. So for example, a couple embracing tenderly and sharing an intense, unspoken, quiet moment is displaying much more intimacy than a couple engaged in sex who only just met and don't know one another well. Exhibitionism isn't intimacy. Nakedness isn't necessarily intimate, either. (Getting undressed in a locker room at the local gym is hardly an intimate act.) Some couples assume that simply living together and sharing the same bed is a form of intimacy. That's not necessarily true, although it can be.

The goal of this secret is to help you realize that with intimacy the whole is greater than the sum of its parts. It's not enough to realize that talking can be a form of intimacy or that affection improves intimacy. You need to see the whole picture and realize that being weak in one area is not something to readily accept. Weakness in any one area will diminish intimacy overall and will probably have a negative impact on other areas of intimacy, too. For example, your low self-disclosure can reduce your partner's sexual affection for you.

If sexual intimacy is sporadic, you may not want to spend as much time together. You will supersize intimacy when you realize that all four pathways to intimacy need to be in good working order. Happy couples don't allow intimacy to fade or lose its luster.

Intimacy in a marriage or in any meaningful loving relationship can be achieved by walking four pathways. Each pathway is important. If any pathway is overlooked, intimacy as a whole diminishes though it isn't eradicated. I call pathways the Four Ts:

- Intimacy through *Thought*
- Intimacy through *Talk*
- Intimacy through *Togetherness*
- Intimacy through *Touch*

Your job is to identify which pathway is weakest for you. To improve resilience in your relationship and have the best-quality intimacy possible, all four pathways need to be strong.

Intimacy Through Thought

I call this "linking by thinking." Some may say that thinking about someone is not intimate, but consider this: Do expectant parents develop intimacy with the baby inside the womb? Undoubtedly they do. Or ask any true lovers who must be separated for a time. Do their thoughts while they are apart link them in any way? Do their thoughts enhance their bonding? Absolutely. Intimacy involves self-disclosure, and this self-disclosure need not always be verbal. Sending our loving thoughts to another is a form of intimacy and it also enhances intimacy. Intimacy always links the people involved in a kind of loving, caring bond.

Happy couples do two things regarding intimacy through thought:

● They make room for each other in their minds; they think about how the other is doing and fill their hearts with positive thoughts about their relationship.
● They replace upsetting thoughts about the other with more positive and realistic ones after an argument or some divisive encounter.

Unhappy couples either don't think of one another during the day when they are apart, or their thoughts are negative. And after an argument they fuel their negative thoughts rather than cultivate a more understanding and forgiving attitude.

Intimacy Through Talk

Several of the secrets in this book will help you to improve the quality of your communication. But by and large, intimacy through talk is all about self-disclosure. The good news is that you can be shy and reserved and not much of a talker but still reveal yourself in ways that increase intimacy. Intimacy through talk is not about the length of your conversation; it's about how well you use the conversation. In order to self-disclose it must be safe for you to do so. A partner who is critical or who gives the message "You're wrong to feel that way" will shut down conversation.

Self-disclosure means revealing what you think and feel about something. To be meaningful and intimate it needs to involve feelings, not just facts. For example, there is a huge difference between saying, "My car needs replacing" and "My car needs replacing but *I'm worried we can't afford it.*" Stating facts says nothing about you. Stating how you feel says a lot about you.

On average, honest self-disclosure in which you reveal your deepest feelings is the most intimate thing you can do. It is far more intimate than having sex. Couples who lack self-disclosure because it leads to arguments or because they are uncomfortable expressing themselves are very vulnerable to breaking up or emotionally detaching from one another.

Intimacy Through Togetherness

It's harder to feel intimate with someone you never see or do anything with. In a marriage, togetherness is crucial. If a couple isn't getting along or if communication skills are inadequate, togetherness can feel like a chore. It isn't enough to breathe the same air. You have to *do* something together, not just *be* together. Date nights or getaways are great ideas. But even ordinary moments at home can be enhanced if you simply pay more attention to each other. Having coffee together can either be a mindless act of sitting near each other while reading a newspaper or watching TV, or it can be an opportunity for a brief conversation. A great way to improve togetherness is to ask yourself this question: "What's it like for my partner to have me around right now?" If your answer is that your partner is bored, irritable, or lonely then you have work to do.

Of course, togetherness must be balanced in some way by separateness. Time alone is also essential for a healthy relationship. Couples often bicker about how much time alone is optimal, especially when one partner wants more time alone than the other. The solution isn't to insist on getting your way. You have to find common ground. It's not an accident that someone who likes personal space often ends up marrying someone who craves togetherness. What seems like a real mismatch really isn't. In fact, the person wanting space would be miserable if he or she married someone who wanted a lot of space, too. The person who craves space is disowning the part of himself that wants more intimacy and closeness. He wants closeness but can't admit to it. But he married someone who will push for more closeness and so he will have it in his life

Intimacy Through Touch

Sex is not the most important part of a marriage but it comes pretty close. It is common for men to feel most at ease using sex as a form of intimacy, while downplaying conversation. The more that practice continues the less connected a woman will feel to her man and she will probably pull away sexually. The man will then feel rejected and push for more sex, prompting the woman to think "He only cares about sex" which isn't precisely true. The average guy who pushes for sex (in an established relationship) is really pushing for a greater closeness with his partner, but it doesn't always appear that way. Physical affection is a crucial part of intimacy through touch. While it's normal for busy couples to give pecks on the lips that aren't always heartfelt and passionate, never lose sight of the need to give and receive regular doses of meaningful affection.

Intimacy after the Kids Arrive

Having children changes forever the face of the marital relationship. When you ask elderly couples what was most meaningful in their lives, most will tell you it was raising their children. Most will say children made their lives fulfilling and worth living. But when you measure marital happiness on a day-in, day-out basis, the evidence is overwhelming: Couples with children are reportedly less happy than childless couples. That is true regardless of age, sex, years of education, religion, race, or income.

One study, "Transitions to Parenthood: His, Hers, and Theirs," published in the *Journal of Family Issues,* showed that marital satisfaction declined within the first six months of a child's life, especially for mothers. By eighteen months, satisfaction had declined for fathers and never recovered until the children left home. Certainly couples with children vary a great deal on their level of happiness, but in general, happiness dips once children arrive. Marital happiness peaks between the honeymoon and the birth of the first child. It reaches a second peak after the children have left the homestead. Evidently, the "empty nest syndrome"—the difficulty parents have adjusting to a childless home—has been overrated. For the majority of couples, marital happiness usually improves when the children grow up and get out.

While the hassles and financial burden of raising children can contribute to dissatisfaction, the main reason for lower satisfaction among couples with children is this: These couples have less time to talk to one another and less leisure time to enjoy together. The couples hardest hit are those with unrealistic expectations of life with children: "I truly believed that having a child meant lullabies, cooing in a rocking chair, and constant 'oohs' and 'ahs' from family and friends. My mother 'oohs,' but I still change the diaper. I can't hear the lullabies for all the crying, and my husband is too tired to do much of anything. And who has time to sit in a goddamned rocking chair?"

About half of all divorces occur within seven years of marriage. One of the many reasons is that the presence of children adds stress and reduces intimacy, which some couples can't easily tolerate. Happy couples succeed at keeping intimacy alive when kids enter the scene while emphasizing the joy that children bring to their lives.

What to Do

☑ *Make sure you have at least fifteen minutes a day of couple time, especially if you have young children.* Don't let this slide. Fatigue and stress increase the odds you'll want more time alone. That's okay but never lose sight of the marriage.

☑ *Add booster shots to your intimacy.* Whatever you're doing that already maintains intimacy, do more of. Go out on more dates or show more affection. Have more sex. Take a few minutes here or there during the day to think lovingly about your partner.

☑ *Self-disclose.* Think of a time from your childhood, happy or sad, and mention it. Make sure you talk about how you felt. Why was that moment important? What impact did it have?

Keep in Mind

♡ Genuine intimacy involves connecting, sharing, and caring.

♡ An intimate moment is measured more by the quality of the overall caring in the relationship than by the intimate act itself.

♡ Build intimacy using all four pathways: intimacy through thought, talk, togetherness, and touch.

♡ Reducing intimacy in one area will automatically reduce it in other areas.

♡ Day-to-day happiness declines when kids arrive, due to added stress and fatigue; but the meaningfulness of one's life increases as does the opportunity for new facets of intimacy to be explored.

Have Creative *("Wow!")* Sex

Craig and his wife, Amanda, sat in the movie theater and watched their favorite stars portray characters that seduced one another with their drop-dead good looks and sexy moves. The on-screen lovers began with a romantic and exciting night on the town followed inexorably by a trip to one of their apartments where they made passionate love for hours. "That's what real lovers do," thought Craig, wishing that he and Amanda could experience that kind of sizzling passion. Amanda thought about the last time she and Craig made love. First they read books in bed, then they cuddled, then they groped, then they had intercourse. In about ten minutes it was all over. Soup to nuts.

Do really happy married couples have sex that lights up the sky like a supernova? Or do really happy couples simply fall into a pattern where sex is, well, okay, but nothing that moves any mountains? Don't unmarried couples, especially those who are just getting to know one another have the best sex of all?

Many think that any fabulous sex that's happening is happening with couples that are single and young. Not so! The truth is that married couples have the most sex and are more sexually satisfied than their unmarried counterparts. The key to having the most sex is having a regular sex partner, and single people are less likely to have such a partner. And while sex with a new partner can be exhilarating because of its newness, the happiest of married couples are no slouches when it comes to creative, heart-pumping, volcano-erupting sex. Sure they have their many ordinary sexual encounters. But the happiest of couples will engage in occasional acts of sexual abandon, too.

What's Your S.Q. (Sex Quotient)?

Could your sex life stand a little improvement? If so, you're not alone. Even the happiest couples get trapped in a sexual funk now and then. Respond to the following to see where you fit in.

1. My partner and I are a pretty close match when it comes to levels of sexual desire.
   False _____ *Somewhat True* _____ *Mostly True* _____

2. I often feel sexually rejected.
   False _____ *Somewhat True* _____ *Mostly True* _____

3. My partner's body and lovemaking style still excite me.
   False _____ *Somewhat True* _____ *Mostly True* _____

4. If I must be totally honest, sex has become mundane.
   False _____ *Somewhat True* _____ *Mostly True* _____

5. I crave more affection from my partner.
   False _____ *Somewhat True* _____ *Mostly True* _____

6. We're not very sexually adventurous.
   False _____ *Somewhat True* _____ *Mostly True* _____

7. Quickies are fun when we have them.
   False _____ *Somewhat True* _____ *Mostly True* _____

8. My partner is willing to please me in ways that I want.
   False _____ *Somewhat True* _____ *Mostly True* _____

9. Sex with my partner creates excitement for me.
   False _____ *Somewhat True* _____ *Mostly True* _____

10. I don't think our relationship is fair.
    False _____ *Somewhat True* _____ *Mostly True* _____

For statements 1, 3, 7, 8, and 9, score one point for False, three points for Somewhat True, and five points for Mostly True. For statements 2, 4, 5, 6, and 10, score five points for False, three points for Somewhat True, and one point for Mostly True.

46–50: Your sex life is satisfying, fun, and creative.

41–45: Your sex life is satisfying overall; occasionally fantastic, occasionally a bit disappointing.

31–40: Your sex life is pleasant but often disappointing.

21–30: Your sex life is bland and routine, occasionally very dissatisfying.

10–20: Your sex life needs a complete make-over.

If you scored below what you hoped for don't be alarmed. Sex for the average couple isn't all fireworks. What is "normal" when it comes to sexual satisfaction may surprise you. A report from the *New England Journal of Medicine* revealed that 20 percent of wives and one-third of husbands from satisfying marriages reported current dissatisfaction with their sexual relationship. (Researchers studied 100 educated couples with an average age of thirty-three.) Forty percent of the men in the study reported occasional erectile or ejaculatory problems. Sixty-three percent of the women reported difficulties with arousal or orgasm (coming too quickly or not quickly enough). Half of the men and 77 percent of the women reported an occasional lack of interest in sex. The frequency of intercourse averaged once a week (one-third reported having sex less than once a week; 10 percent had sex less than once a month). Evidently, mild sexual frustrations and occasional loss of sexual interest are par for the course in most marriages. However, that doesn't mean that better sex isn't an option. The truth is that the happiest couples find ways to go the extra mile in pleasing each other sexually, at least once in a while. You can, too.

Hot Intimacy

Hot intimacy is the term I use to describe what busy couples (who isn't?) can do to add spice and pizzazz to their ordinary encounters. Hot intimacy lets couples go from warm to hot in sixty seconds or less. Hot intimacy doesn't necessarily last long—it might be as brief as a kiss—but it conveys a passion and a sizzle that otherwise might be missing.

Hot intimacy doesn't necessarily involve sex but it certainly inspires sex. The formula for hot intimacy is to take any ordinary warm encounter you might have with your spouse and add something to it that makes it sizzle. Hot intimacy is fun. You know you've tapped into the power of hot intimacy when it makes you giggle or laugh.

For example, if you're walking through the mall together "warm intimacy" might be holding hands. Hot intimacy might be a sudden passionate kiss in the middle of the lingerie aisle. (Remember, hot intimacy isn't about exhibitionism; it's about being spontaneous and playful.) Many couples think about taking a shower together. But the logistics can get complicated, especially if you have young children wandering about needing your attention. So instead of showering together, do a kind of tag-team approach. You step out of the shower just as your partner is about to step in. Hand off the soap or a towel, get in a few quick grabs and smooches, and you've added a little zest to what might have been an ordinary moment.

If sex has been a sore subject and your partner won't take kindly to any hot intimacy that smacks of sex, keep it fun and playful but nonsexual. For example, hot chocolate on a cold night might be "warm intimacy." You can warm it up even more by starting a fire in the fireplace or stepping outdoors together and gazing at the stars in the night sky.

Hot intimacy works best for couples who get along but whose lives have become too hectic. It allows for moments of passion when spare time is at a premium. The more sexually aggressive partner should keep in mind that hot intimacy involving too much grabbing or overt sexuality might be a turnoff to your partner. Focus instead on the romantic side of things, not merely the sexual. Make hugs and embraces tender and long lasting; kiss her with your eyes as well as your mouth; tell her how beautiful she is. Send love notes or flirt online with one another (assuming you each have your own computer).

The Question of Quickies

Some people regard a "quickie" as a poor substitute for making love. Many women view them as opportunities for the man to get sexual relief but not for them to. That's because women usually require more tenderness and foreplay before they are ready to appreciate intercourse. But happy couples will enjoy a quickie now and then. It isn't that a rapid sexual encounter creates happiness; rather, happy couples tend to be more playful sexually and will be inclined to have a fast, spontaneous lovemaking session just for the fun of it or because it might be indiscreet.

If you or your partner has an unfavorable opinion of quickies, check to see if you are unhappy in other areas of the relationship. If you feel taken for granted or unappreciated, for example, any kind of slam-bam sex might hit that nerve and therefore not be something you'd enjoy. If quickies aren't enjoyable because the woman needs more time to get aroused, keep in mind that foreplay isn't just physical stimulation. Most women will be turned on by acts of thoughtfulness, tender (nonsexual) affection, sincere compliments, flirtatiousness, and anything a man can do just to help her relax. If a man does those things often enough, a woman might need less time to get sexually aroused and quickies could become a fun addition to your sex life for moments when time is limited.

Wow Sex

Okay, there is no way to give you tantalizing tips on creative sexual maneuvers in just a paragraph or two. But you know how to get that information. Books abound to help loving couples get their creative juices flowing and the Internet is a vast resource of methods and ideas. It's less important *what* you do; it's vitally important that you *want* to do something different. Different isn't necessarily kinky. Different means out of the ordinary for you. You just have to make a pact with your spouse that you will indeed do something different—not just next time but for many next times. Your goal is to elevate your sex life so that it becomes even more exciting and something you look forward to more than you already do.

What to Do

☑ *Pick one sexual fantasy and start there.* There is probably some sexual act you enjoy most. Make sure you mention it and emphasize it. Be explicit. If it is something you've never tried but only fantasized about, well, *ask!* Your spouse might be more than willing to accommodate you.

☑ *Don't make love in the same place twice in a row.* Get creative. Changing locations really can make a difference.

☑ *Purchase a sophisticated video on improving your love life.* Forget the X-rated videos with idiotic plot lines. There are tastefully made films designed to show couples, very explicitly, new or imaginative ways to enhance their sex life. Watching them will definitely be a turn-on but the truth is you just might learn something, too.

☑ *Have sex without orgasm.* If that seems impossible, then have sex and delay orgasm as long as possible. The goal is to enhance sensual and sexual pleasure in non-orgasmic ways. Couples who focus on the climax often fail to fully enjoy all that sex has to offer. Now is the time to appreciate other bodily sensations and take long, lingering minutes doing things you'd ordinarily skip quickly over.

☑ *Plan a sex date.* Pick a day and time and start talking about details. What exactly will you do? How will you do it? What surprises might you have in store? Make plans a day or two in advance and give each other tantalizing reminders that whet your appetites.

☑ *Do something different each time.* Simply plan on doing something—anything—that's different every time you make love. It needn't be exotic or acrobatic, just different.

Keep in Mind

♡ Even happy couples can have sex lives that are at times mediocre. But happy couples don't take mediocre sex lying down. They find ways to get imaginative and playful.

♡ Couples wanting to spice up their sex life can start by taking ordinary warm moments of intimacy and occasionally adding extra spices.

♡ Doing something different—almost anything—from the usual sexual routine will probably make your next love-making encounter playful and memorable.

♡ If your sex life is very dissatisfying it probably means that other aspects of your relationship aren't working either. Make sure you improve those other areas before you try to improve your sexual relationship.

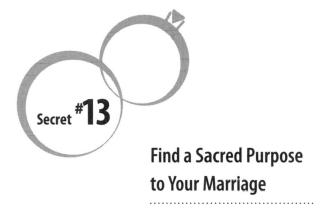

Secret #13

Find a Sacred Purpose
to Your Marriage

Imagine an object that is so precious, so sacred, it must be locked away for periods of time so that it won't get broken or stolen. The object's essence—whatever it is that makes the object precious—remains, despite the fact that the object is hidden away.

What if you believed that your marriage—as it is right now, no matter how it is displayed—is sacred? If you really believed that, what would you do differently? How would you view your spouse? How would you interpret the fact that occasionally you are not happy within the relationship? If you believe that your marriage is sacred, then all problems and difficulties must be viewed from that light.

When the artwork in Michelangelo's Sistine Chapel was faded and discolored by hundreds of years of exposure to air and pollutants, it was very carefully repaired and preserved. What do you do when your marriage has lost its color? If you view the marriage as sacred, not merely a social institution, you will have no choice but to do all you can to preserve it and help it regain its previous splendor.

If you embraced the belief that your marriage really is sacred, you would think the following:

- God, or however you think of a greater power, has a purpose in mind for your marriage. That purpose, broadly speaking, involves you growing spiritually.
- Problems you encounter are opportunities for spiritual growth. For example, failing to achieve something you want is an opportunity to experience humility; being hurt is an opportunity to learn forgiveness; doing harm is an opportunity to be forgiven.
- No sadness will lead to despair; no anger will lead to bitterness or contempt; no disappointment will lead to discouragement.
- An emphasis on gratitude clears away resentments and bitterness.

The word "sacred" is sometimes misspelled or mistyped as "scared." That is a meaningful coincidence. It can be quite scary to embrace the idea that your marriage is sacred, because it will undoubtedly compel you to change some of your ways of relating. You can't simply blame your spouse anymore for those times you are unhappy. If your marriage is sacred you have an obligation to deal with marital problems squarely and with respect, humility, and compassion. If you are scared, you will deal with problems by avoidance or by excessive hostility and blaming.

Seek Holiness or Happiness?

This entire book is about how to increase happiness in your marriage. But there is no cookbook formula to provide you with happiness. There are formulas to teach you how to act with more love, respect, compassion, and optimism; and by following them, your chance of experiencing marital happiness will greatly increase. Happiness can never be achieved directly; rather, it is a by-product of the kind of life you lead. Happiness is not dependent so much on what happens to you; it depends on how you deal with what happens to you.

Each of the thirty secrets in this book is designed to make you a better spouse, certainly a better person. By seeking to be a very good person, your marriage will improve, as will your ability to experience joy.

Be Willing to Self-Sacrifice

Most married people will readily admit the sacrifices they make for their spouse. They point to their obligations ("I work so hard for you") or the minor aggravations they must learn to endure. But one must be willing to make deeper sacrifices, too; sacrifices that actually cost you something. Marriage is either sacrificial or superficial. You can't always compromise and find some comfortable middle road. Sometimes one spouse must give up something completely in order for the other to get what they want. For example, what does a couple do if a career promotion means relocating to a place one spouse doesn't want to go to? Who makes the sacrifice? The point is that someone must. And the sacrifice should not ever be made with a sneering "You owe me!" attitude. You don't need to sacrifice your values or your safety. A spouse with your best interests in mind wouldn't ask you to.

Does it mean you must put up with *anything* in your marriage? After twenty-plus years as a therapist witnessing people's marriages, I do believe that some marriages should end. Certainly marriages in which abuse of any kind continues should end. But sadly, most divorces happen because the couple drifted apart. In other words, many of those divorces didn't have to happen. Drifting apart happens when you lose sight of one another; when at least one of you stops showing devotion; when self-concerns continually override concern for the other.

Viewing your marriage as sacred will prompt you to halt the drifting apart process before it goes too far.

What to Do

☑ *Make a list.* Write out all the things you would say, think, and do differently if you fully believed that your marriage is sacred. Can you start making those changes?

☑ *If you have religious or spiritual beliefs, attend some kind of service more often.* For many of us, religious services are a once-in-a-while ritual at best. If you've been thinking about attending more frequently, why not try it for a few months? To improve motivation, attend a service that other friends will be attending. Get together for coffee or breakfast afterward.

☑ *Select some personal virtue you'd like to enhance and make a pact with yourself to improve upon it for the next several weeks.* Since nobody is perfect, improvement is possible. Perhaps you wish to show more honesty, compassion, tolerance, gratitude, or kindness. Daily self-reminders can keep you on track. If you'd prefer, make it a family project. Young children can learn more about virtuous behavior and in the process the family unit can be strengthened.

☑ *If you have an inter-faith marriage, don't allow differences in dogma to diminish caring, intimacy, and family involvement.* You can participate in some of your spouse's religious rituals—if appropriate to the ceremony—without renouncing your own beliefs. Or, if you prefer, you can participate in the preparation for those rituals—baking certain foods, purchasing gifts, etc. You can ask your children questions about their religious education classes without challenging what they've been taught. You can express your differing views to the children in a manner that shows acceptance of what they've been taught. Religious differences don't have to make a difference.

Keep in Mind

♡ If you start viewing your marriage as sacred you will undoubtedly become aware of self-improvements you need to start making now.

♡ Religion and spirituality become more important in life the older you become.

♡ Research findings suggest that adding a dose of religion or prayer to your daily routine won't hurt and may help.

♡ A devotion to spiritual concerns may not improve happiness or fairness in your life, but it can make your life more meaningful.

Secret #**14**

Boost Commitment

Do you lie in bed at night secure in your partner's commitment to you? Or do nagging doubts—her flirtatiousness, his aloofness—disturb your rest?

When commitment to a relationship is weakened, the amount of love and trust in the relationship is diminished. You may consider yourselves the best of friends, but remember this: Friends aren't usually fully committed to one another (though they do care). If your best friend takes a job 2,000 miles away, you may remain friends, but it's unlikely you'll pack up and relocate, too. If your best friend betrays you, or simply develops interests divergent from your own, you may stop spending so much time together. In a committed relationship, that doesn't happen.

Only in a committed relationship can you risk being fully intimate. When you doubt your partner's degree of commitment, you may walk on tiptoe, trying not to disturb him. You'll start second-guessing him—saying and doing only those things you think he'll appreciate and love you for. But you won't be yourself. And you'll never know whether he's hanging around because he wants you or the image you've created.

When you doubt your own degree of commitment, you'll hold back from giving fully to the relationship. But your holding back can have negative consequences of its own—diminished intimacy, caring, and companionship—which can lower your happiness and further unravel your sense of commitment.

Should You Stay Committed to an Unhappy Marriage?

Happy couples have a belief that the marriage is sacred and that one's partner is dependable. They don't view commitment as a chain that binds people together but rather as a willingness to persevere when times get rough.

"The thought of divorce never enters my mind," one man told me. "I'm not always happy with my wife. But that's when my commitment to her means something."

At first, commitment may well be a by-product of a satisfying relationship; partners commit because they are happy together. But thereafter commitment is a force of its own. Commitment leads to further happiness as much as happiness leads to further commitment.

You may make a commitment because a relationship is working. But then you must keep your commitment in order to keep your relationship working. Commitment is a promise to hang in there, to keep investing in the relationship despite boredom, hurt, or the uncertainty of it all. Commitment is an agreement to be unhappy once in a while.

How would you feel if your mate promised "I'll stay with you as long as . . ."? Or even worse: "I'll stay with you . . . until

I change my mind." Some marriages, certainly, should end. We all deserve more from life than remaining in a unhappy relationship. But a commitment with a list of qualifiers is something less than a commitment. "What I wanted was a commitment," said one woman, disturbed by her fiancé's comment that if he got the right job offer he would relocate with her or without her. "But what he gave me was a commitment with an asterisk."

Three Types of Commitment

The first type I call *empty commitment.* In this case the couple is committed not out of love and devotion but out of dependency or obligation. They stay together because they have to. If the focus is only on grim obligation or mutual dependency, that couple may never rise to a higher level of commitment.

A second type is *romantic commitment.* It is the same as saying "I'm committed to you because I love you." This level is based on attraction and requires happiness to be sustained. As soon as happiness diminishes or attractiveness wanes, commitment dries up. It is a feeling-based commitment, but feelings can and do fluctuate.

The final type is *moral/spiritual commitment.* It assumes that feelings of love can go up and down but that devotion to one another is valuable and honorable. It is a commitment not just to the partner but also to the vows. It is a commitment to each other's growth. About 20 percent of all divorces occur within the first two years of marriage. Nearly 40 percent of divorces happen by the fourth year of marriage. Younger couples in particular don't seem to wait until they're miserable before they divorce. Probably because they are young and attractive alternatives are still available, divorce seems like a reasonable option compared to sticking it out.

If your marriage is falling apart, it's understandable that you might no longer fully commit yourself to it. At such times, as long as some shred of hope exists, it can be helpful to commit—not to the relationship but to working on improving the relationship. Choose a time frame acceptable to each of you (one week, one month, six months) and devote yourself to marital improvements. Commitment:

- Provides us with something to hold on to when so much else in this world seems so chancy and unpredictable.
- Is more than a promise. It is a devotion to that promise.
- Has value precisely because reasons will always exist not to honor it.
- Is a decision to love, and a decision to maintain that love despite obstacles.

It isn't easy remaining committed when your relationship hurts. But being able to withstand and resolve marital problems requires such a commitment.

What to Do

☑ *Do yourself and your spouse a favor: verbally state your commitment from time to time.* This need not be a formal renewal of vows, although that might be nice. When making changes to improve the relationship, do so with the clear statement that such changes reflect deeper commitment. Spouses often say, "I love you" or "I miss you" but rarely acknowledge, "I'm committed to you." Once in a while, that's important to hear.

☑ *If you sense you are less committed to the relationship than your mate (but wish to be more committed) resolve to* act *more committed one day at a time.* Before you fall asleep at night, and right after you awaken in the morning, tell yourself you will act *as if* you were a fully committed partner for that day. Don't make the mistake of waiting until you *feel* more committed before you *act* committed. There is no better way to generate stronger feelings than to act in ways consistent with those feelings. If you act uncommitted, you'll feel uncommitted.

☑ *If you are more committed to the relationship than your partner (and are worried and frustrated by his stance), devote more energy to activities* outside of the relationship *that are personally fulfilling.* As psychologists remind us, an over-focus on the marriage by the more committed partner can actually *lower* the other's commitment even more. The less committed partner may feel pushed or smothered (and back away for more space), and will devalue the need for personal commitment because he is confident the other will never leave. Besides, if you are overinvolved trying to get your mate to be more committed, you are probably underinvolved in other important areas of your life.

☑ *Don't use commitment as a bargaining tool.* Commitment is non-negotiable. Keep in mind these two "nevers": NEVER make idle threats about separation or divorce. Even if your marriage is in trouble, flippant remarks of "Why keep trying, let's just end it" corrode the core of the relationship. NEVER sleep in separate beds as a way to punish your mate or display anger. Sleeping together is symbolic of faith and commitment.

☑ *Make two lists: the events that would diminish your desire to remain committed (such as an affair), and the events that would sustain or strengthen your commitment.* Discuss these with your mate. Determine whether you could take any steps that would strengthen your commitment. Understand that some reasons for commitment (such as security of the children) are not based on love alone.

Keep in Mind

♡ Commitment is always a decision to act that way.

♡ You can act committed without feeling committed.

♡ Commitment is not a one-time decision. It is ongoing. Every effort to work through a difficult time is really a decision to recommit to the relationship.

♡ The more committed you are, the longer and harder you'll persist through tough times. Success rarely occurs without persistence.

Secret #15

Get a Healthy Perspective on Your Family of Origin

Did you ever wish that your entire family was the inspiration for a Norman Rockwell painting? Imagine everyone getting together for a holiday, full of love and merriment, warming their hands in front of the hearth on a snowy day. The children—decorated with hot-cocoa mustaches—dart about the country home like rabbits. Friends drop by bearing cookies and fruitcake, shaking the snow from their coats. You can almost smell the turkey and the minty, evergreen wreath; you can almost hear the laughter, the crumpling of the wrappings; everything and everybody mixing together as smoothly as hot butter into cream . . .

Well, maybe next year.

As appealing as it may be, most of us would be grateful for much less during the holidays. Appreciative children, a friendly phone call, a small but festive meal together, cheery music—we don't ask for much, and often we don't even get that.

Holidays are special times for families, complicated by strained family relationships. When warm embraces and hot toddies are replaced by forced smiles and bickering, you can feel grateful when the whole damn day is over and done with.

But leaving your parents and siblings behind after a hard holiday won't make you more content with life. Unresolved family issues stay with you and keep you discontented. You can't resolve those problems by ignoring them or living far away from them.

Family Affairs

When did you first feel grown up? After graduation? When you got married? After receiving your first paycheck from a "real" job? Those may be indications of adulthood. But two indications of maturity are: First, viewing your parents realistically—not as perfect, not as totally toxic—but as people with their own strengths and weaknesses. When you can view your parents as they are, not as they once were or how you'd like them to be, you've grown up a bit more. A second indication of maturity is the ability to be true to yourself (and less anxious) in your family's presence. That remains being able to say "yes," "no," and "ouch." It means no longer pretending that all in the family is okay if it is not okay.

When you get married, it's important to distance yourself from your parents and family somewhat. There is a natural need to bond with your mate, to have room to grow, to become a cohesive twosome, independent from your original families. Remaining connected to your family of origin is important (particularly if you have a supportive, caring family), but the real work is to consolidate your relationship with your spouse. Once that is accomplished (and it could take several years), you reconnect to your family in a different way—less as a son or daughter, more as an adult. Couples on the extreme—either too involved with their original families or too disconnected—will eventually have problems.

Janine came from a "close" family. The three grown daughters had such a positive relationship with their mother that they kept nothing from her. No secret, no marital issue, no personal problem was private where Mom was concerned. Dad loved them too, but of course he was a man, on the periphery of the family, involved in masculine endeavors. What did he know?

The family problems were many. Mom and Dad had a polite relationship, but that was all. Mom confided in Janine often about her lonely life with Dad, "If I didn't have you to talk with, Janine, I don't know what I'd do." After Janine married, her husband, Mike, did all he could do to convince her to live in an apartment. She wanted them to live with her parents (to save money, of course). Within a year, Mike had grown tired of the many nights they spent at Janine's parents. Weekends were especially difficult. Sunday afternoons were reserved for her family, and that was that. So Mike did what any red-blooded American boy would do: He took up golf. Soon Janine spent more time confiding in Mom about her faltering relationship with Mike than she spent with Mike. Shortly before their third anniversary, Mike and Janine separated.

In Janine's case, having a close family choked off her relationship with her husband.

Will had a different relationship with his parents: None. He wanted as little to do with them as possible, and he had good reasons. So when he >>>

> > > married Rochelle, all was wonderful for a while. But Will's problem was his ambivalence about being close to someone. In one sense, he felt very needy for love, trying to fill the hole left open by his uncaring parents. But he also was frightened of too much closeness. After all, the closer you get, the more deeply you could be hurt. With Rochelle, he'd demand closeness; sensitive to the slightest rejection on her part yet indifferent to her needs. He gave and took, but only on his terms.

Disconnecting yourself from your original family—even for understandable reasons—often leaves you hungry for love but unwilling to expose yourself to being hurt. Your relationships move in fits and starts, never satisfying for long, thereby increasing your need for—and fear of—love.

If you've been hurt by your parents, disconnecting from them for a period of time can be a useful and necessary step in the process of healing. Confrontations may also be necessary. But resolution doesn't happen if you are held prisoner by your anger. Your parents may never change. They may never understand your hurt. They may never express remorse. But totally disconnecting from them, or connecting with them only in anger, won't heal you or make you feel closer to your mate.

If you are too close to or too distant from your parents, your goal is to connect with them and to be in emotional contact with them without struggling to change them. That means you must let them be who they are. You don't have to like it. You don't have to put up with it. But you do have to accept the way things are. You may have to grieve that your relationship with them will never be better than it already is. You deserved more from your parents, and they failed you in some important way. That's unfair. That's sad. And that's reality. When you let go of your unmet expectations of your parents, you can get on with your life more happily and productively.

If you are too enmeshed with your family of origin or if you are too detached, you can bet that your spouse will soon fail to meet your expectations. Too much unhealthy involvement with your family (they have too much say over your life or you give them too much power) will lead you to feel your spouse has let you down. Your spouse might rebel and want less time with your family. Or you may start to feel that your spouse isn't as warm as your family is. You'll think that your partner doesn't understand you or care about you the way your family does.

If you are distant from your family you might feel abandoned or slighted when your partner wants to spend time with his or her family. Or you might become possessive. Or, craving a sense of family, you might immerse yourself in your spouse's family but lose a sense of your own individuality. You might feel like an adult child, still needing parents to guide you.

The goal is to maintain a healthy balance: Keep connected to your family if possible (assuming they are not abusive or toxic) but maintain your own individual, marital, and family life, too.

What to Do

☑ *Don't feel guilty if you need to set boundaries.* For example, if your folks like to drop by unannounced and that's a problem for you or your spouse, it's okay to ask your folks to call first. It's wonderful to have a "My home is your home" philosophy but you and your spouse also need privacy. You can always tell your parents to call or stop by anytime during those times when you know it won't be inconvenient.

☑ *Focus less on what a parent does to bother you and pay more attention to how you respond.* Think of what happens between you and your parent as a dance. It takes two of you to keep the dance going. Changing your response to a parent's predictable ways can help alter the dance pattern. How do you ordinarily respond? Rehearse a different response. If confrontation never helped, ignoring provocative behaviors might (but stay consistent—ignoring one unkind remark but exploding after the fifth is not a significant change). If you always debate your parent, try listening with empathy ("Sounds like you're feeling hurt, Mom"). Even if your response doesn't work the way you'd like, your main goal is to respond less automatically and with more thought. It is your knee-jerk reactions (even if they are nonverbal) that need altering. Don't defend yourself against unfair accusations or subtle criticisms. Responding "I'm sorry you feel that way" or "That's interesting" keeps you balanced and in control.

☑ *Connect with each parent (or sibling) separately.* On the telephone, be sure to talk with each parent. (One parent being the spokesperson for both can add distance to your relationship with the other.) In person, try to arrange for time alone with each parent or sibling. Take a walk with your father. Help

Mom prepare a meal. Connecting with family members only as a group diminishes one-on-one intimacy.

☑ *Limit conversations about an absent family member.* When relationships are strained, there is a tendency to converse with a parent about other family members instead of keeping the focus only on the two of you. Some discussion of others is normal. But take time to ask, "How are *you* doing?" And don't get sidetracked.

☑ *If the relationship with one or both parents is highly conflicted, and reasonable "adult" dialogues go nowhere, write a letter to the parent detailing your hurt and anger.* Be as specific as possible, but don't mail it. It provides some cathartic relief, clarifies your issues, and can better prepare you for any future discussions. A letter of this kind can be especially helpful if a parent is deceased.

☑ *To better understand your parents, talk to your aunts and uncles about them.* (Holidays and birthdays are convenient times to do this.) Ask them what it was like for your parents when they were growing up. Don't complain to a relative, especially if you believe that relative will inform your parents. Indirect messages are not helpful.

☑ *Don't agree to keep secrets if doing so divides your family loyalty.* Except for a surprise birthday party, it is *never* a good idea to agree to keep a secret from your mate. Secrets disrupt family communication and worsen pre-existing problems. (Common secrets include health issues, pregnancies, affairs, financial woes, etc.) Since only some family members are in on the secret, they have to speak cautiously around those not in on the secret. Consequently, pre-existing problems worsen as the anxiety level elevates. While you might be intrigued by family gossip, never promise to keep secrets that will make you uncomfortable. If someone tells you a secret before you have a chance to protest, you don't have to keep the secret if it makes you uncomfortable. That's the secret-teller's problem, not yours. Refusing to keep secrets is disruptive to the family at first. But it helps keep you sane.

Keep in Mind

♡ Staying connected to your family does not mean putting up with abuse. You can detach—as much as you need to protect yourself—but still remain connected.

♡ We usually expect our partners to make up for what we didn't get growing up. Since our partners are not responsible for our happiness, we'll eventually blame them for our discontent.

♡ Forgiving a parent is good and healing, but may not be your next step. Recognizing your anger and hurt and seeing its merit, rather than pretending you shouldn't feel the way you do, must occur first.

PART TWO

*Decreasing
the
Negatives*

Stop Judging (and Start Accepting)

Jennifer was upset with Joe. Really upset. "Why didn't you stand up for me when your mother insulted me?"

"I didn't think you needed my help," Joe said.

"How could you think that? Couldn't you see how hurt I was? I was practically in tears."

"I think—"

"No that's the trouble. You never think. You just act the way that's easiest for you. I don't think it matters to you how I feel."

"Of course it matters," Joe interjected.

"That's not the sign of someone who loves his wife. You were being a coward. When will you grow up and stop being intimidated by your mother? Are you so weak you can't even defend me when your mother is out of line?"

Two things were going wrong with this exchange. First, it was escalating. Having an argument, even a loud argument, isn't necessarily a sign that a couple is mishandling the conversation or that their relationship is headed for disaster. But arguments that *escalate* do predict unhappiness. Second, Jennifer was attacking Joe. Maybe she had a right to be upset but her verbal attacks intensified. She went from "You never think" to "I don't think it matters to you how I feel . . . You're a coward . . . grow up." She was vilifying Joe and she was digging in her heels, refusing to understand his side of the story.

Everybody judges others to some extent. It's a very human thing to do. But there's a difference between making a judgment and being judgmental.

It's appropriate to say, "I don't like this." That's making a judgment. When you are judgmental you are finding fault with the other person without really understanding that person fully or understanding your part in the problem. The use of strong, negative labels ("You're lazy . . . You're irresponsible . . . " and other put-downs) indicates that someone is being judgmental. A judgmental attack almost always leads to defensiveness by the attackee, and the conversation goes nowhere. A judgmental person doesn't consider alternative explanations for why something happened. Usually, judgmental people have many blind spots—certainly they are blind to many of their own shortcomings.

Still, it's not easy to never be judgmental. It's a human weakness. If you want your relationship to succeed and be happy, judgmental remarks need to be minimized.

Levels of Criticism

In his book, *After the Fight,* psychologist Daniel Wile outlines five levels of criticisms. The higher the level, the more the criticism is an attack and the more defensive or despairing the attacked person will feel:

1. Criticizing behaviors
2. Criticizing feelings
3. Criticizing character
4. Making accusatory interpretations
5. Criticizing intentions

Jennifer first criticized Joe's behavior. She didn't like that he stood by while she was being insulted by his mother. She quickly escalated her attack by criticizing his intentions, telling him he didn't care about her feelings and only did what was easiest for him. She made an accusatory interpretation when she told him he was intimidated by his mother. (Had he denied it, she would have told him he was *unconsciously* intimidated, which, of course, would be impossible for him to disprove.) Then she insulted his character by calling him a coward and telling him to grow up.

Any criticism, even if it is a polite criticism of another's behavior ("You forgot to mail that letter") will almost always be followed by some defensive, and possibly accusatory, remark ("I was in a hurry. Why didn't you remind me to mail it?"). But as criticisms escalate, defensiveness will be strong and so will hurt feelings and resentment.

When arguments escalate, it's common to get annoyed and even outraged that a partner is defensive. In fact, "You're getting defensive!" is just another attack, as if the defensive person is wrong to act that way. If you went out in the rain without an umbrella and became indignant that you got wet, people would ask, "What did you expect?" It's the same with arguments. If you criticize your partner, certainly if you go on the attack, your partner will get defensive. What did you expect?

There is no way to prevent defensiveness. The use of the now famous "I" statement, such as "I'm angry you're not paying attention to what I'm saying," won't help much. An "I" statement is supposed to be a comment on the speaker's thoughts and feelings and not an accusation of the person being spoken to. A "You" statement, such as, "You aren't listening to me!" is an accusation. But some "I" statements are really disguised "You" statements. The person on the receiving end of such an "I" statement still gets defensive.

Since it is humanly impossible to avoid saying things that will make a partner defensive, your goals are twofold: Criticize behaviors, not the essence, of the other person; and understand that defensiveness is normal especially when one is attacked. By understanding that defensiveness happens, you won't get mad when it occurs and have yet another thing to be critical about.

Learn to Accept One Another

Acceptance is a tricky, yet vitally important attitude. It doesn't mean you can't complain or request that your partner make certain changes. But it means you might have to accept that not all changes will happen the way you want. You have to accept your partner for who he or she is even if certain traits annoy you. A relationship in which some annoying behaviors aren't changed at least somewhat won't be satisfying. But a relationship without some degree of acceptance won't last.

Acceptance should not be a grim resignation. It is really a gift of love; at the least it is a peace offering, a surrender to a certain truth that your partner is fundamentally the way he or she is and that certain changes won't happen the way you'd like. Yes, every annoying flaw in your partner *appears* changeable. You tell yourself that since you don't act a certain way, certainly your partner can stop—by sheer willpower—acting that way, too. And when your partner doesn't stop, you view him or her as being stubborn, defiant, or uncaring. Instead of insisting that your partner change, can you change your desire to get your partner to change? No? It isn't that easy to change, is it?

Acceptance isn't impossible. We do it every time the weather is bad and we must cancel our plans. We do it when we get through another birthday even though we might dislike the aging process. We accept that many things are simply the way they are. That outlook is important in a marriage, too.

If you are having difficulty peacefully accepting a partner's flaws, consider that some of your difficulty is caused by you. When you unrealistically demand that your partner make certain fundamental changes incompatible with who he or she really is, he or she will inevitably get mad, argue, or feel that the relationship isn't fair. Bad feelings will grow. If you ever do "accept," it will be with an attitude of bitter defeat, not with an attitude of peaceful co-existence, which is what you need.

What to Do

☑ *Appreciate what qualities of yourself your partner has had to learn to accept.* By understanding that you too yearn to be accepted, you might find it easier to accept your partner.

☑ *Discover the beneficial aspects of your mate's annoying qualities.* An always-on-the go partner can make your life more adventurous. A quiet partner might be a strong anchor in times of hardship. An overemotional spouse might allow you to experience emotional expressiveness in a manner you don't feel comfortable doing but perhaps need. A spouse who hates to spend money will probably save money and you'll have it handy when you really need it.

☑ *Don't allow yourself to read negatively into a partner's motivations and actions.* Emphasize the behaviors you don't like and try not to demonize your partner's character or motives.

☑ *Relax and practice "acceptance affirmations."* Choose something about your partner you don't like. Lie down, relax, and tell yourself "I accept that he . . . " Tell yourself repeatedly, "I don't like it but I accept it." If you are having a hard time accepting it, say, "I accept I can't easily accept it." You should notice that after many minutes of this, you'll feel lighter and more accepting.

Keep in Mind

♡ Criticizing another's behaviors is better than criticizing another's character.

♡ Criticism, however justified, almost always causes defensiveness. Expect that and don't become indignant when the person you're criticizing gets defensive.

♡ "I" statements aren't as helpful as previously thought. Use them if you can but don't expect them to be the basis of a productive, mature dialogue.

♡ Ultimately you must learn to patiently accept some of your partner's less than desirable qualities.

♡ To accept another is not to like what the person does; acceptance is a willingness not to emotionally oppose things that probably won't change.

Reduce Your Need to Be Right

Mark didn't like the way his wife, Connie, disciplined their children. He thought she was too lenient. He also thought she spent money a bit too frivolously. When they talked about these differences it wasn't like listening to two teammates trying to figure out the best strategy to win the game. It was like listening to a school principal talk down to a student. Mark always used flawless logic to express his opinion and since he was obviously "right" his wife, Connie, was obviously wrong.

Using the logic of "But I'm right!" as a means to get your way is the oldest game in the book. It is usually a bad move for two reasons. First, most things couples disagree about have no absolute right or wrong answer. Differences are usually based on opinions and subjective interpretations, not scientific facts. Second, the need to be right carries with it a dismissive attitude toward one's partner. Even if you are, in fact, right, relationships involve a give and a take. Both sides need to be considered and respected. Getting along is not about getting your way. It's about sharing, compromise, and finding common ground.

People who need to be right are actually being controlling, perhaps dictatorial, and often a tad selfish, but hide behind "I'm right!" to justify getting their way. People who need to be right are often excellent debaters and their partners are less adept at debating. But the outcome of living with a partner who always has to be right is usually one of two things: a couple who butt heads constantly in a battle of wills; or a relationship that is more parent-child than adult–adult. Parent-child relationships are usually highly unsatisfying for both people. The controlling person (parent) may get his way but often feels rejected in other ways (often sexually) since the child spouse doesn't feel a lot of warmth and is unlikely to show much affection. Spouses who need to be right win a lot of battles but they lose the war. That is, their relationship suffers as a result.

Does Your Partner Have an "I Know Best" Personality?

There is nothing wrong with having a strong opinion about something. In fact, if the topic is important and you feel very strongly, you should voice that opinion. But when a spouse always "knows best," conversations aren't about solving problems but about getting one's way. It can be confusing to you at times if your partner is someone who has to get his or her way. It's confusing because your spouse can be adept at making you feel wrong to have the opinions you do. Over time, you may actually doubt your own judgment and defer even more to your spouse. But when that happens you are like a flower bud that is closing up, not blossoming. Once your spirit closes up you will feel depressed, ineffective, insecure, and self-critical and the marriage will never be more than what it is already. How do you know if your partner is a control freak who must always be right?

- She debates you on insignificant issues. Your relationship always feels competitive.
- If you try to get your way you are accused of being controlling or demanding; if he tries to get his way it's because he's right.
- Your mistakes are pounced upon; her mistakes are to be overlooked.
- You don't feel understood or cared about.
- You give in a lot because to try to get your way just leads to a long battle.
- When you do get your way you must appreciate your partner's "sacrifice." He will feel owed and have a bad attitude. If you were to act that way you would be called childish.

The Causes of the "I Know Best" Personality

The causes are many and varied. Statistically, more men than women have an "I must be right!" personality. Why? A large part of that is social conditioning. Women are conditioned by society, much more than men, to be accommodating people pleasers. Men, more so than women, are trained to compete and win. Also, a female child who is abused, neglected, or made to feel bad about herself often becomes more depressed and somewhat unassertive as an adult. A male child who is abused or made to feel bad about himself may also become depressed or unassertive as an adult but more often develops a kind of arrogance and narcissism. The narcissism is really a defense against feeling unworthy. But this narcissism can show up as an insistence on being right.

Often, people with this quality had parents who made them feel wrong and not good enough. To be right is to be good enough. So such a person needs to be right so he or she will feel worthy, good enough, and loveable.

Some people get this way because as children they had to take on adult responsibilities at an earlier age. They learned to fend for themselves and not rely on others to give to them. Talking about issues never got them anywhere so they are not the best communicators. They do what they have to do to get by and dislike being challenged. Ironically, they want more closeness since they had to forgo some of that growing up. But they push closeness and intimacy away by their need to always be right.

. . . .

? Did You Know?

That partners in a relationship strive to bring about balance when the relationship feels unfair? If one partner has a great deal of obvious power (gets his or her way; makes demands; can overrule the other; and so on) the other partner will learn to develop "hidden" power. Hidden power usually shows up in ways that are rejecting or annoying to the more controlling partner. For example, if the overtly controlling partner has strict rules about spending, the covertly controlling partner will often limit sex or affection. There are many ways that a spouse who feels unfairly treated can "stick it" to the more controlling partner. Those ways can be conscious or unconscious. The point is that there is always a price to pay for unfairness. The "winner" eventually "loses."

Some people with careers where they exert a lot of authority (notably police or corrections officers; military personnel; physicians; and so on) have a greater tendency to take their work attitudes home with them and get caught up in the trap of having to be right much of the time. When the need to be right is accompanied (as it usually is) by a difficulty showing much tenderness and warmth, a spouse stops feeling cherished and the emotional gap between them widens.

What to Do

☑ *Realize that fairness and goodwill is more important than being right.* Your relationship will work if it is based on mutual respect and consideration, not one-upmanship.

☑ *Realize that your insistence on being right is a cover for deeper feelings of unworthiness or inadequacy.* You may not believe that, at least not right away. But at least consider the possibility that what's motivating your insistence on being right isn't just the merits of your arguments but something else. If you try to uncover what might be the deeper motivation, you might stop trying to be right long enough for your mate to finally feel heard.

☑ *If you and your mate get locked into frequent battles of will, agree to flip a coin when you can't reach an agreement.* Flipping a coin ensures fairness and ends debate. It isn't ideal but it might teach you that a give and take (not a take and take) is essential for a marriage to work.

☑ *Locate the deeper worry or concern that is often underneath your stated opinion.* For example, if you disagree about parenting, speak about your fears of what might happen if parenting is mishandled. Make your concerns the topic of conversation, not what you must do about those concerns. Then hear out your partner. What are his or her underlying concerns? Now try to come up with "solutions" that address each of your concerns. Forget about what is right. Focus on what works.

Keep in Mind

♡ The need to always be right and get your way is controlling. You are using "logic" to hide behind your need to have things go your way.

♡ The need to be right creates a one-up/one-down style of relationship. That will not be rewarding in the long run. Mature couples want a relationship of equals.

♡ The need to be right suggests a narcissistic personality. Narcissism is often a defense against feelings of unworthiness.

♡ The more you get your way overtly, the more your partner will try to get his or her way covertly.

♡ To be right all the time is to see things through competitive eyes. You and your spouse should not be adversaries but teammates.

Secret #**18**

Don't Expect Miracles Overnight

Michelle and Dan didn't want a major overhaul of their marriage. They were committed to the relationship but a little impatient with one another. Progress in making minor improvements had gone into a skid recently, and each felt the other was being a tad uncooperative.

Michelle wanted Dan to cut back on his overtime hours and to occasionally give the baby her 3 A.M. bottle. Dan wanted a little more lovemaking, "Since the baby was born we're down to once a fortnight. Isn't that below the national average?" He also didn't want her to make their social plans without giving him a few days' notice.

"Before I see you next week," I said at the end of our meeting, "I'd like you to do something you may think a bit odd." Their curiosity piqued, I told them, "Between now and next time I'd like you to sleep on opposite sides of your bed, to switch positions. It's a small change, insignificant really, but I'm interested in any effects it may have."

The following week they reported the surprising results.

"I couldn't get comfortable at all," Michelle said. "On nights I was exhausted I'd fall into bed only to realize I had to switch sides." **> > >**

> > >   "It didn't feel right to me either. In fact, last night we changed back. But interestingly, we made love three times this week. Something about being on a different side of the bed seemed more . . . provocative."

From that small exercise Michelle and Dan realized that even small changes can be awkward and that improvements in the marriage can come from unexpected places, if one remains open to the idea of change.

The Road to Improvement

Which of the following attitudes do you think is realistic regarding efforts to improve one's marriage?

If a person really wants to change, willpower—not techniques—is all that's required.

The hardest part is getting started. Then it gets easier.

No one expects change overnight, but if significant progress isn't made within a few weeks, the person isn't trying hard enough.

If progress is followed by a reversal to old patterns of behaving, then the technique didn't really work.

If you answered "None of the above" you're correct. None is realistic. Let's look at each statement and see why.

If a person really wants to change, willpower—not techniques—is all that's required. All of us have heard of people who've changed bad habits without fuss or fanfare—they lost weight and kept it off with no fad dieting, or they stopped smoking "cold turkey." But most people change their ways in fits and starts with a good deal of backsliding. Willpower is important, but without helpful strategies to stay on course, frustration and hopelessness can set in.

The hardest part is getting started. Then it gets easier. In my experience with couples, the hardest part about improving the relationship is not making changes. Rather, maintaining those changes is where couples need the most help. Sometimes partners set immediate goals too high—a setup for failure. Sometimes progress by one partner creates, paradoxically, anger in the other. "Yes, I know he's made improvements," one woman said, "but I keep thinking, 'It's too little too late.' Why didn't he change five years ago when I first asked him?" Sometimes positive changes result in unwanted side effects, such as when a couple with no leisure time together make more time—only to spend some of it arguing. Maintaining positive changes is very possible. People succeed in it every day. But it takes time and is often cumbersome. Without helpful guidelines, even spicing up your love life can leave you with a touch of indigestion.

If significant progress isn't made within a few weeks, the person isn't trying hard enough. What do we mean by "significant progress"? Some habits, like placing dirty clothes in a hamper instead of on the floor, can happen soon and are easy to monitor. Other changes, such as a husband who makes efforts to be more devoted, can take time to develop and are not always apparent.

If progress is followed by a reversal to old patterns of behaving, then the technique didn't really work. Think again. The technique did work for a while, but the new habit hasn't yet taken hold.

When making relationship improvements, it's essential to understand that partners' actions mutually affect one another. If you take some improvements—yours or your mate's—for granted, the new changes will have less holding power because you've stopped encouraging them. As old patterns return, you and your partner can get critical and discouraged, which can add to your difficulties.

Five Ways You Might Sabotage Your Partner's Change Efforts

There is a term in biology called *homeostasis*. It refers to the tendency of certain biological processes to resist change and maintain the status quo. For example, if you are overheated (a negative change), you will start to perspire, which will help cool you down (a return to the status quo). If you are injured and bleeding your body will try to get the blood to coagulate so you can stop bleeding and start healing. Anyone who has ever struggled with weight loss has experienced homeostasis firsthand. As you lose weight your body tries to maintain the status quo by making it harder for you to lose more weight and easier for you to regain weight. Homeostasis shows up in relationships, too.

Linda wanted her husband, Bill, to say he loved her more often and to come up with ideas on what to do together for fun. First Bill resisted her efforts to get him to change (homeostasis was in full gear). Then he decided that she was right and he began saying more sweet things and coming up > > >

>>> with weekend plans she'd enjoy. But when he did these things Linda responded unenthusiastically. She resented it had taken him so long to make the changes and wasn't about to jump for joy the minute he finally did what he should have done all along. But because her response wasn't positive, Bill lost interest and the couple resumed their usual pattern of relating. The forces of "change" lost and the forces of "stay-the-same" won.

People who want their spouse to change for the better commonly succumb to the force of homeostasis and actually sabotage their partner's efforts to change. There are five common ways they do that:

1. *Not showing any enthusiasm or even mild pleasure when a partner starts to make desired changes.* Find a way to make some positive response even if you are annoyed that it took so long for your mate to step up to the plate and change. It isn't easy breaking old patterns. A positive response is not only inherently rewarding but it also gives feedback to your mate she is on the right track.

2. *Insisting that a partner change "for the right reasons . . . don't do it for me but do it because it's the right thing to do."* Don't confuse the issue by discussing your partner's underlying motivation to change. Give him credit for making the effort even if it isn't his instinct to change that way on his own.

3. *Responding to a positive change by piling on demands for additional changes.* Take it a step at a time. Appreciate the changes that have started before you read off the list of additional improvements you want.

4. *Never softening your hard edges.* When a partner tries to make changes, don't remain irritable, cold, or distant. Warm up! Show some affection or make thoughtful gestures. If you find it hard to rid yourself of your hard edges, that's an indication that making personal change is indeed hard at times. Cut your spouse some slack if you have trouble making personal changes, too.

5. *Believing that the changes made will make you happy and content.* What happens if your mate makes the necessary changes and you're still not that happy? Don't automatically look for more reasons to blame your spouse. Look inward and see if perhaps you are dissatisfied with yourself in some way. Unless a spouse's actions are completely obnoxious or abusive, insisting that she make changes suggests you might have an underlying dissatisfaction with something or someone other than your spouse.

Realistically, improvements in marital happiness proceed like a bullish stock market. The trend over a week or a month is positive—gains are made—but some days show a decline. Care to take stock of your marriage?

What to Do

☑ *Follow the "Thirty Day Rule."* Give one another at least that long to make a noticeable (not necessarily an ideal) improvement.

Abandoning efforts before thirty days reflects an unrealistic view of what the change process involves. If progress has been made by day thirty, keep at it. You're doing something right.

☑ *Appreciate changes by your spouse even if his or her heart isn't in it (yet).* Changes in attitude often follow long after those in behavior. Typically, a spouse bent on improving her relationship wants two things from her husband: for him to make changes and for him to *want* to make changes. Consequently, when he grudgingly agrees to certain requests, she may respond, "Forget it. You have a lousy attitude." In happy marriages spouses occasionally do things they don't like to please their mates. When your partner pouts, tell him, "I know it isn't what you'd prefer, but it means a lot to me that you're doing it."

☑ *Minimize displays of impatience and criticism when progress seems slow.* In a crisis, or after prolonged and repeated failures at improvement, many couples don't tolerate struggles to try harder. They want the problem *eliminated*. Now. Even patient partners can grow weary when progress is punctuated by slow-downs and setbacks. At the first sign of mounting impatience, take a piece of paper; each of you should draw a line down the middle, and put your names on top—one on each side. Down the left-side column, mark the date. At the end of every day, each of you is to grade yourself and your partner on your efforts at improvement. There is to be *no discussion* about the grades for the next thirty days. This exercise provides you with important feedback from your mate without the added risk of an angry debate that might detour progress.

☑ *Predict obstacles to improvement.* Ask yourself, "What could happen in the next few weeks that would slow me down or make me want to give up altogether?" Discuss your answers with your partner. Knowing in advance that a bad day at work, an illness, or spousal criticism can deter progress is good preventative planning.

☑ *Know what to say or do when you don't know what to say or do anymore.* For example, if you find yourself faltering for no apparent reason, or if you can't find the right words to soothe a spouse frustrated by slow progress, say this: "I know I'm not doing my share and I'm sure you've noticed. I don't want this to be happening. Can you bear with me?" Or more generally, "I don't want to say or do the wrong thing but I'm not sure I'll succeed. Please don't take it personally." Such comments demonstrate an awareness of your difficulties, sensitivity to your spouse's feelings, and a desire to improve. Consequently, your spouse may be supportive instead of critical.

☑ *Make goals as specific as possible.* Wanting your spouse to "respect" you is too vague. It's better to say, "I want you not to criticize me in front of company." One helpful guideline here is to imagine that your partner doesn't understand English very well. Vague requests like "more time together, more affection, more caring" are less clear than "I want us to go on a date twice a month" or "I want you to put your arm around me when we watch television" or "I'd like to play tennis once a week without you resenting it."

Keep in Mind:

♡ Don't minimize the small changes. They are the foundation for bigger ones.

♡ Understand that once changes have been made there is a tendency to relax, to "take your eye off the ball"—and for old patterns to re-emerge.

♡ Changing chronic ways of relating, especially if there is pressure to improve quickly, creates anxiety. It's uncomfortable but not fatal, and if it's not too intense it can spur on improvements rather than impede them.

♡ Nobody is perfect, and even irritating characteristics—however annoying—are part and parcel of the person you fell in love with.

Secret #19

Be Less Accommodating of Hurtful Behaviors

Doug and Millie lived together for two years before they got married. No obvious problems emerged while living together so marriage seemed like the right step to take. But six months into the marriage Doug started to go out with his buddies a lot more. Millie felt a bit neglected but didn't strenuously object because any time she voiced a concern Doug told her to stop acting like his mother. Soon Doug was getting drunk at least once every weekend. When Millie complained Doug told her she was making problems out of nothing, so she kept quiet after that.

When the couple finally came to see me they had been married for four years. Doug continued to abuse alcohol regularly but never admitted it was a problem. Much of the couple's free time was not spent doing things together. Doug spent most of his time with his pals. Intimacy at all levels was low: They communicated poorly, sex and affection were absent for long stretches, and "togetherness" was a foreign concept.

The problems were many but issues had begun in part because Millie was willing to tolerate Doug's actions that she considered hurtful and neglectful.

The truth is that efforts to be "nice" can backfire in a relationship if you have to adapt to your spouse's negative and upsetting behaviors.

Why Tolerating Negativity Leads to Unhappiness

First of all, let's be clear about what constitutes "negative" actions. Annoying habits such as knuckle-cracking or inborn personality traits such as shyness or being a "night person" may be inconvenient or mildly irritating but they don't really constitute the kind of negativity that can ruin a marriage. Negativity refers to persistent levels of irritability, harshness, rudeness, selfishness, hostility, withdrawal, and other such actions. Everybody will act in those ways occasionally and one shouldn't pounce on a spouse just because he or she is having a bad day. In fact, **Secret #2** to a happy marriage is the ability to give a spouse the benefit of the doubt. But when negativity is frequent enough to make you feel hurt, mistreated, unloved, or unappreciated, overlooking it is a mistake.

When you adapt to a spouse's negativity a predictable series of events takes place. First, you become frustrated or hurt. Then you become resentful. Eventually you start judging your spouse's character more negatively and it's hard to give him credit when he does something nice. You start to think negatively about him even when you're not together. That causes your overall level of "liking" him to fall. As you like him less you withdraw from him more. Now there is less togetherness, perhaps more arguments, and a tendency to start leading parallel lives.

Tolerating negativity is like tolerating a little poison ivy in your garden.

Of course, marriages and relationships are complicated. For example, it is possible that you have accommodated more spousal negativity than you should have to but because of many other good things about the relationship, the relationship is okay. But is "okay" good enough to define the quality of your marriage? How about "comfortable" or "fine" or "good"? Are those the words you really want to best describe your marriage? Why not happy, fulfilling, beautiful, loving? If you set very modest goals, don't be surprised if you achieve them.

Dr. Gottman's research suggests that one reason some couples who make improvements in their marriage suffer major setbacks is that they didn't lower the barometer for detecting negativity. In other words, couples that backslide, even if they are doing more positive behaviors and fewer negative ones, are still tolerating higher levels of negativity than they should. Over time, such a tolerance creates ill will and emotional detachment.

Are You Too Nice?

Being too nice is not a nice quality. It lends itself to your becoming a martyr over time (remember, most martyrs in biblical times were burned at the stake or eaten by lions) and feeling resentful, maybe even bitter, depressed, and certainly unappreciated. Kindness is necessary in life if we want to get along with people. But it isn't healthy to accept and tolerate routine unkind behavior from your spouse.

Dr. John Gottman at the University of Washington studied newlywed couples and wanted to determine the qualities displayed early in the marriage that predict which couples would be happy later on, divorced, or still married but unhappy. A large factor was the wife's ability to detect lower levels of negativity from her husband early on and speak up about it. Couples who later divorced or who unhappily remained together had wives who adapted to negativity from their husbands by letting some negative actions persist and grow.

Clues You're Too Nice

How negative should you let something get before you speak up about it? Generally speaking, the moment the negativity starts to bother you in some way it needs to be addressed. People who wait until matters have gotten out of hand are described as follows:

- They are peacemakers, uneasy about stirring up conflict.
- They are like ostriches, putting their heads in the sand and hoping the negativity will just go away on its own.
- They confuse legitimate complaints with "bitching."
- They confuse passively adapting to negativity with being understanding and compassionate.
- They don't view themselves as equals.
- They only feel entitled to complain after a long list of hurts has accrued or their pain gets too great.

Making a complaint is a recognition that you're starting to feel hurt and that you deserve better than that.

But What about Acceptance?

Any person you live with—especially a spouse—is bound to occasionally do some things that bother the heck out of you. And that person will occasionally be mean, selfish, whiny, unfair, and any other adjective you might come up with. To accept the person doesn't mean you will not speak up if some negativity is bothering you. It means you will not reject the person outright for acting that way. It means recognizing that no one is perfect and some level of negativity will always exist to varying degrees. But once the negativity bothers you it's important to talk about it and do something about it. You may not be able to eradicate the negativity but talking about it might help you make it far less bothersome.

Acceptance is a two-way street. If a partner is always grouchy, critical, and fault finding, and insists that you accept her the way she is, then she is failing to accept you. To accept you she must consider that you don't like those qualities of hers and that she should modify them to fit better with your needs.

When your relationship is truly based on love then yes, you will accept your partner despite his or her flaws. But your

❓ Did You Know?

There is a simple way to tell the difference between being unassertive (not speaking up when you should) and being understanding (not objecting to negative behavior out of kindness or compassion). When you are being genuinely nice and not operating from fear, you feel good about not complaining. When you are not complaining because you're being unassertive, you will feel anxious or frustrated.

partner will endeavor, out of love, to minimize any actions that are hurtful.

What to Do

☑ *Have a "speak up hour."* If you and your mate have too many petty criticisms of each other (or, if you rarely complain but wish you were more assertive), schedule a "speak up hour" once a week. The rule is that each of you is allowed to express your annoyance about things you might otherwise ignore. Don't make pejorative comments ("You're lazy"). Instead, say "I'd prefer it if you would . . ." This might force you to raise complaints you might otherwise keep to yourself and nip problems in the bud.

☑ *Distinguish between negativity you know you can easily live with and negativity you know will bother you if it isn't corrected.* Hoping that a bothersome behavior will "go away in time" is a clue that you might be tolerating something you shouldn't.

☑ *Locate someone who, to you, is a role model for proper assertiveness.* By asking yourself, "What would (this person) do in my situation?" you can give yourself the courage to speak up if need be.

☑ *Keep in mind that your spouse telling you "No" isn't necessarily a bad thing or a negative thing.* Your first reaction might be that your spouse isn't cooperative when you are told "No." But maybe your spouse really is busy or your request is not a good idea. For example, if your spouse says "No, I can't make love tonight, I'm too busy with the kids," you are better off trying to find ways to ease your spouse's burdens—not just that day but in days and weeks to come. He or she might in fact be overwhelmed and exhausted. Stop complaining and start helping out more. In time, "No" will turn into a vibrant "YES!"

Keep in Mind

♡ Adapting to unacceptable behavior is never a good idea.

♡ On average, it's better to err in the direction of complaining too soon than complaining too late.

♡ Adapting to negative behaviors sets off a domino effect whereby annoyance leads to resentment, which leads to unstated hostility, which leads to demonizing your partner, which leads to emotional detachment and relationship failure.

♡ Being nice and positive is deadly to your relationship if it means putting up with behaviors that are hurtful.

Secret #20

Stop Arguing about Problems That Will Never Go Completely Away

A large number of couples come into my office hoping to put an end—once and for all—to certain arguments that keep recurring. "We just don't see eye to eye on this," one spouse might tell me. And often they look to me to be the final decision maker; to inform them who is wrong and who is right and halt their perpetual, "Here we go again!" disagreements.

Which of the following statements do you think are, for the most part, true?

- If a couple cannot resolve their differences then at least one partner is being stubborn or selfish.
- If a couple has between two and four differences that they cannot resolve, it's a strong indication the partners are simply incompatible.
- All differences can be resolved if the couple is patient and considerate enough.
- Failure to resolve an ongoing problem is an indication that communication skills probably need improvement.

● When a couple is hopelessly at a standstill on a divisive issue, they have only two options: grudgingly accept a partner's view or keep pushing to get their own way.

If you strongly believe that any of the above statements is true then you may be headed for unnecessary trouble in your relationship. The truth is that every couple has at least one, and probably four or five, differences between them that will *never* go away and will *always* be a source of tension or aggravation. This is due to differences in personality, as well as lifestyle wants and needs. For example, if one person is a die-hard sports enthusiast and his partner isn't, then that couple will most likely have frequent disagreements about time (and money) spent on sports. If one partner loves to socialize and the other prefers more solitary activities, disagreements in that area will erupt from time to time. But believe it or not, such differences are not a problem.

Temporary Solutions to Permanent Problems

There are helpful ways for couples to handle perpetual differences. But they involve adopting a positive attitude about those differences. If your differences and disagreements cause you to view the relationship as unfair or unhealthy then you will never be able to truly manage and "put up with" those differences. Instead, you will be plotting ways to do away with them once and for all. The three best attitudes to adopt are:

1. Personality differences are permanent. They can be adjusted or tweaked but not eliminated.

2. If I flexibly and fairly allow for differences to exist, each of us will be happier.
3. If I left my partner for someone with a different personality, I'd be exchanging one set of permanent disagreements for another.

It is the persistent effort to force a partner to change certain personality traits that is poisonous to a relationship, not the fact that there are differences.

When a couple gets into a periodic tug-of-war, each partner feels like a victim. The feeling of victimization compels each of them to get more stubborn and uncompromising, which just fuels their mutual sense of unfairness. Partners are no longer viewed fondly but quite negatively. Once you view a partner in the most negative light and your differences polarize you, the relationship appears seriously flawed and fantasies about how to escape the marriage start to show up more often.

Once you develop a more positive attitude about the differences between you and your spouse, those differences must be managed. Think of it as similar to adjusting to a climate where once in a while it gets unbearably hot or cold or rainy. You may not like it but if that is where you choose to live then you will learn to adapt. It's inconvenient at times but the benefits of living there outweigh the costs of moving to a new location. (And if you did choose to move to a new climate you would face a new set of disappointments. Perhaps the climate is quite comfortable but there is overcrowding or the cost of living is high or you're too far from friends and family. Perfect contentment is rare.)

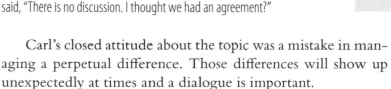

Carl and Melinda disagree about spending. He likes to save as much as possible and finds most expenditures other than food frivolous. Melinda likes to buy things for their home that may not be absolutely essential but make for a lifestyle that pleases her. At one point Melinda said she would not spend any more money on household items for at least three months. Two weeks later she found an antique piece that was exactly the kind of item she had been searching for, for the past year. She wanted to buy it. When she spoke to Carl about it he said, "There is no discussion. I thought we had an agreement?"

Carl's closed attitude about the topic was a mistake in managing a perpetual difference. Those differences will show up unexpectedly at times and a dialogue is important.

When the same old disagreements arise, couples should approach the problem by asking, "How do we want to handle it this time?" That attitude reveals an acceptance that the differences will appear now and then, as well as a willingness to try to cooperate and find common ground when they do. Sometimes one person must completely give in to another. Sometimes the solution will be a temporary compromise. Whatever the answer that day, the couple knows it's just a matter of time before they'll have to face the issue another day.

Did You Know?

Researchers estimate about 70 percent of all couples' arguments are about perpetual, "unsolvable" problems. If couples learned to stop trying to eliminate their differences and instead manage them more fairly and effectively, most would experience a dramatic reduction in arguments, leading to an increase in cooperation, goodwill, and a sense of friendship.

What to Do

☑ *Develop a sense of humor over your differences.* Learning to laugh occasionally about your differences can make all the difference in the world. For example, one couple often disagreed about how frequently they should have sex. The wife thought her husband was oversexed. He had two T-shirts printed. Her T-shirt read "All men are . . . " and his T-shirt read "ANIMALS." Occasionally they wore the shirts together in public. Joking about their differences eased much of the strain.

☑ *Appreciate the benefits of your differences.* Chances are your partner's ways expose you to certain life experiences. Perhaps your differences balance each other out in some vital way.

☑ *Refuse to make the other person wrong.* Halt the angry debates. Have your debates and efforts to persuade really helped? Ultimately you must compromise and agree to disagree. Start with that attitude and eliminate the combativeness. It will save you energy and improve goodwill.

Keep in Mind

♡ Every couple will have differences in personality or lifestyle choices that will never completely go away.

♡ The effort to eliminate those differences causes more dis-ruption in a relationship than the differences themselves.

♡ Strive to be fair.

♡ Your differences will be less annoying if you can find some humor in them.

Uncover and Reduce
Hidden Agendas

"They're *my* parents, Gina. I don't want to visit them. I don't want to call them. We've been over this a dozen times already. Can't you just drop it?"

"I still don't understand why you won't even call your mother on her birthday, Lee. You've hardly spoken with her in five years. Don't you think it's time somebody put aside their pride . . ."

"Why can't you stay out of this?" Lee interrupted. "I told you, they're my parents, not yours. I don't tell you how to run your relationship with your parents, so why do you insist on running my relationship with my parents?"

"That's just it," Gina said. "You don't have a relationship with your parents. Can't you see that?"

"This is going nowhere," Lee concluded, walking out of the room.

Lee believed that if Gina would just view the problem from his perspective, she'd back off. But the problem wasn't Gina's lack of understanding or her stubbornness. And the problem, despite what Gina believed, wasn't Lee's relationship with his parents. The real reason Lee and Gina argued periodically about this problem—to no avail—was because they weren't arguing about what they *thought* they were arguing about. Misidentifying the fundamental problem made it impossible to resolve.

You're Not Always Fighting for the Reasons You Think

"What worries you about Lee's unwillingness to speak to his parents?" I asked Gina one day.

"They are his parents. A son shouldn't simply cut himself off from his parents no matter what they've done to him," Gina answered.

"But how does his decision to cut himself off from his family affect you personally?" I probed.

"It doesn't," she began. "But maybe I worry that if he can close himself off from his parents, he'll close himself off from me one day. Let's face it, we began marriage counseling because we've drifted apart the past two years."

"So it sounds to me that the reason you argue with him about his relationship with his parents is because it symbolizes something more important—his relationship with you. Deep down, you worry that he might stop loving you, too."

"Yes, that's right," she said.

"I never realized that before," Lee commented. Lee never realized it because it was *hidden*. Hidden agendas crop up from time to time in a relationship. But for happy couples the hidden agendas don't stay hidden for long.

Hidden agendas begin as doubts or fears one spouse has about the other's level of commitment or caring. Here are some examples of one spouse voicing a request or comment, and the other spouse's thoughts in response to it:

> *Spouse A:* "Let's ask the Pattersons to join us for dinner."
> *Spouse B:* The Pattersons? Doesn't she want to spend time alone with me?

> *Spouse A:* "We can't afford a piano. Besides, you know I've been waiting years to buy a backyard pool."
> *Spouse B:* He always gets his own way. Don't my wishes count?

> *Spouse A:* "Good night."
> *Spouse B:* Already? I thought we'd have time to chat before going to bed. Isn't he interested in knowing how my day went?

> *Spouse A:* "Dear (*cough*), would you bring me the vaporizer (*gag*), please?"
> *Spouse B:* She can't fool me. Her cold isn't that bad. That's just her way of avoiding sex.

Hidden agendas are the unstated undercurrents to a superficial dialogue. The undercurrents might be conscious or unconscious concerns, so it isn't always easy to unearth them. If a person forms a negative, unstated interpretation of his partner's behavior ("She's avoiding sex because she doesn't find me attractive"), he will subsequently interpret many of his partner's innocent behaviors as avoidance ("She wants to phone her sister? I've heard that excuse before . . ."). Left unspoken, hidden agendas build hurt and frustration and couples end up arguing over seemingly unimportant matters. For example:

> *"Why must you always call your sister?"*
> *"What? I don't always call my sister. And it's a local call, so what's the big deal?"*

The big deal is the meaning he gives to his wife calling her sister. But that meaning (his fear that she's avoiding sex with him), if left hidden, will complicate their relationship unnecessarily.

Three Kinds of Hidden Agendas

Researcher John Gottman and associates say that hidden agendas are about three fundamental issues:

1. *Love and worthwhileness.* Does my spouse care about me? Love me? Trust me?
2. *Responsiveness.* Is my mate interested in my thoughts, feelings, wishes? Am I sexually appealing? Does he or she value my opinions? Can I talk to him or her about my feelings and wants without being criticized?
3. *Status.* Am I in a one-down position to my mate? Do his or her needs always come first?

Whether you're arguing about money, children, in-laws, or what to eat for dinner, if you're fighting that same old fight, then hidden agendas may be lurking.

The Influence of Your Past

Your hidden agendas may have little to do with your current relationship issues and more to do with your past. For example, if you felt rejected or unloved as a child, you might worry about that in your marriage even though there is no basis for it. You may overreact to minor personal slights or read into neutral events as evidence of rejection. If your former lover cheated on you, your levels of trust might be low and insecurity high. So if your partner arrives home an hour later than expected you might have an argument over the fact that he never called to say he would be late. But what's motivating your anger is not his lack of consideration or forgetfulness but your fear he might be seeing another woman. Left unstated, he might think you're making mountains out of molehills.

Once you uncover your hidden fears it's best to report them without being accusatory. For example, it's better to state to your spouse in a matter-of-fact way: "When you come home late without calling I start to feel insecure because of my last relationship. I need you to keep me informed." That tone is not accusatory and offers a suggestion for future action.

What to Do

☑ *Call a "Time Out" during a tiresome argument and try to determine your hidden agenda.* Ask each other, "Are you worried or hurt because I'm not showing you enough love or caring? Are you hurt because I'm not taking an interest in you? Are you hurt because you feel controlled or powerless?" Once uncovered, allow the one with the hidden agenda to speak uninterrupted. Don't challenge or debate his or her views. Every thirty seconds or so, summarize what you've heard to be sure you've understood correctly. If you respond to your partner's uncovered agenda with anger, insensitivity, or impatience, you'll fuel the original fear (fear of being unloved, uncared for, or controlled).

☑ *Send a signal.* If you have difficulty revealing your hidden agenda during conversations or arguments, have a prearranged signal that will indicate to your spouse how you really feel. For example, a pillow placed outside and on top of the bedspread may signal that you are wondering if your partner finds you attractive or is interested in things important to you. A lighted candle may signal your doubts about being loved and cherished. Such symbols make your feelings known in a quiet but effective way, without accusation, and reflect your continued desire to improve the relationship.

☑ *Once your hidden agenda is revealed, agree with your mate that for the next two weeks you will call attention to behavior that sparks your hidden agenda.* For example, if your agenda has to do with status and equal power in the relationship, inform your spouse every time you believe she is doing something that lowers your status. (You will notice those behaviors anyway. Calling attention to them gives your mate immediate feedback about his behavior and reduces the odds that your resentment will build.) The purpose is not to debate whether or not you are right and your mate is wrong. The goal is to clarify when your hidden agendas are being sparked so that the two of you can work together with understanding.

☑ *Ask yourself "What did I want from my childhood (or former relationship) but did not really get?"* Did you want more security? Love? Guidance? Interaction? Influence? Whatever your answer, look to see if those needs are not currently met. They may be the source of your hidden agendas.

Keep in Mind

♡ Arguments over "little things" are about bigger agendas.

♡ The three kinds of hidden agendas (caring, interest, and status) reflect fundamental needs in life: the need for love, self-esteem, and control (influence). Once uncovered, treat those needs with respect.

♡ You can help your mate uncover his or her hidden agendas by being less defensive when they are pointed out. Remember, revealing a hidden agenda is not an accusation. It is an explanation of one's feelings.

♡ Unresolved childhood wounds are often a source of hidden agendas in your current relationships.

Secret #22

Don't Allow Arguments to Escalate

One hallmark of couples that usually end up unhappy is that their arguments tend to escalate until one person eventually withdraws in contempt. Arguments by definition are unpleasant affairs. But when they escalate it sets in motion a series of events and attitudes that can undermine future relationship happiness. When arguments escalate:

- Odds increase that one person will say or do something very hurtful that is not quickly forgotten.
- Future conversations are limited for fear of starting another argument.
- The desire to self-disclose during calm periods diminishes as one's partner is viewed as attacking or unsympathetic.
- Ill will develops and bad attitudes linger.
- The argument itself is unlikely to get settled fairly.
- There will be a greater likelihood that the next tense discussion will have a harsher start-up, thereby increasing the odds of another escalating argument.

So as you can see, if you and your mate are like most couples you probably cannot afford to have escalating arguments. The goal is to notice when matters are starting to heat up and immediately take steps to de-escalate.

The Heat of the Moment

If you use air conditioning in your home you know that your air conditioner has a sensor that tells it how hot or cool a room is. If the room reaches a certain "hot point" the air conditioner kicks on to cool the room. That is precisely the kind of thing that needs to happen during conflict with your spouse. Before the conflict gets too hot, one of you must turn on the air conditioning, so to speak, and cool things off between you.

There are several steps you can take to help make it easier to keep arguments from escalating.

Start Gently

Keep this phrase in mind: "Harsh and jarring leads to sparring." When the first minutes of a conversation are harsh, an escalation is very likely. According to John Gottman, author of *The Marriage Clinic: A Scientifically Based Marital Therapy,* women are much more likely to start disagreements more harshly than men and men are more likely to stonewall. This may be because women are usually more aware of and frustrated by relationship problems than are men. Still, a harsh start-up will more than likely lead to a quick escalation (or to the man shutting down from the conversation altogether.) It's often a mistake to start a discussion that sounds accusatory, such as "Why did you . . . ? Why couldn't you . . . ? Why won't you . . . ? How could you . . . ?" and so on. If you find yourself asking such questions, try to rephrase them in the form of a statement. So the accusing question, "Why do you have to treat the kids that way?" might become, "I'm concerned about the way I see you treat the kids." The second statement still carries a bit of a punch but it is far less attacking.

It is easier to have a gentler conversational start-up if your attitude about your spouse going in to the discussion is already favorable. If you are disgusted by your spouse in some way or cannot seem to give him or her the benefit of the doubt in situations (see **Secret #2**), it will be harder to start conversations gently.

Downshift Sooner than Later

Obviously, as the tension levels rise so does the ugliness of the conversation. Don't wait until matters have gotten out of hand before you try to fix the conversation. As soon as you notice that your levels of hurt or anger have reached about a number 4 on a scale of 0 to 10 (10 being the most hurt or angry), you need to start de-escalating. This isn't always possible because sometimes anger spikes to a high level rather suddenly.

Downshifting usually involves doing one of two things. First, you can help calm the moment by pointing out that what your partner is saying has merit. So you might say things like, "That's a good point . . . I never thought of it that way before . . . I can see why you feel the way you do . . . You're right . . . That's worth thinking about . . . " and so forth. Second, you can help repair a conversation that's breaking by pointing out your own errors. You might say, "I shouldn't have said that . . . I was wrong to say that . . . Let me start again . . . I didn't mean that, let me try again . . . I'm sorry . . . " and so on. It isn't a good idea to follow any of those helpful comments with the word "but." Don't say, "You have a good point BUT . . . " or "I shouldn't have said that BUT . . . " The use of the word "but" diminishes what you are trying to accomplish.

Cooperate When Your Partner Tries to De-Escalate

This step is crucial. If your partner tries to downshift an argument but you refuse to cooperate, the argument will only escalate again or your partner will withdraw. Whenever you hear your partner say things like "You're right about that . . . I'm sorry . . . " your next thought should not be "Damn right I'm right!" but instead should be "Oh, he's trying to calm us down. Good. Let me help."

If your partner isn't cooperating with your attempt to calm things down, ask for his or her cooperation. Your partner may not have realized that was what you were trying to do. Say, "I'm trying to get us to calm down. Can you help with that?" Your spouse is likely to go along especially if you had spoken earlier about your need to de-escalate future conflicts.

What to Do

☑ *Rehearse de-escalating.* Pick a topic that used to be controversial but isn't anymore, or make one up and pretend to have different opinions. Your goal is to try to have your usual argument/discussion but this time pay attention to how it escalates and take steps to de-escalate. This suggestion is very important. If you just try to wait until you have a real argument and hope for the best you will likely be disappointed. Better to practice changing those patterns when cooler heads prevail.

☑ *Remain seated during arguments.* Just that simple step can actually keep discussions from getting out of hand.

☑ *Hold hands during a heated discussion.* It's harder to escalate when you are holding hands.

Keep in Mind

♡ De-escalating conflict is probably the most important skill you need to learn to be a successful couple.

♡ In a pinch, use either of these two-word phrases to de-escalate an argument: "You're right . . . I'm sorry."

♡ If your partner tries to calm down a heated discussion, cooperate.

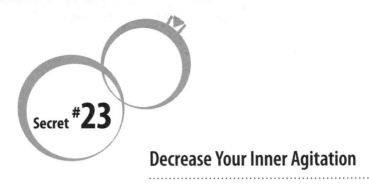

Secret #23

Decrease Your Inner Agitation

Most days when Fred came home from work he was in a bad mood. It wasn't fun for his family as he'd often snap at them and find things to complain about that really weren't that important.

If he and his wife had a tiff he'd walk away and sulk. Then he'd spend his time going over their argument and thinking about ways he was right and she was wrong, which only made him more agitated. Fred never really learned to calm down.

Learning how to calm down might make all the difference in the world in your relationship.

Your Calmness Quotient

Take the following quiz. Place a check mark next to how often you feel the statement is true for you.

1. I'm usually pretty easy going.
   Rarely _____ *Sometimes* _____ *Most of the Time* _____

2. When I come home at the end of the day I need to have peace and quiet.
   Rarely _____ *Sometimes* _____ *Most of the Time* _____

3. Slow checkout lines and lousy drivers really annoy me.
   Rarely _____ *Sometimes* _____ *Most of the Time* _____

4. When my spouse is upset I get very physically tense.
   Rarely _____ *Sometimes* _____ *Most of the Time* _____

5. I can continue a dialogue when the conversation gets tense.
   Rarely _____ *Sometimes* _____ *Most of the Time* _____

6. I find it easy to relax.
   Rarely _____ *Sometimes* _____ *Most of the Time* _____

7. After my spouse does something I really don't like I stew about what he or she did wrong.
   Rarely _____ *Sometimes* _____ *Most of the Time* _____

8. I'm described by others as patient and tolerant.
   Rarely _____ *Sometimes* _____ *Most of the Time* _____

9. At least once a week I "fly off the handle."
   Rarely _____ *Sometimes* _____ *Most of the Time* _____

10. I don't require others to behave well in order for me to feel relaxed.
    Rarely _____ *Sometimes* _____ *Most of the Time* _____

For numbers 1, 5, 6, 8, and 10, score one point for Rarely, three points for Sometimes, and five points for Most of the Time. For numbers 2, 3, 4, 7, and 9, score five points for Rarely, three points for Sometimes, and one point for Most of the Time.

44–50: You are a calm person and unlikely to let negative emotions get the better of you.

37–43: You handle conflict well most of the time but occasionally feel inner turmoil you cannot let go of easily.

30–36: You are more easygoing than not, but have a lot of inner tension.

23–29: You are usually tense and agitated and have to work at staying calm.

22 or below: You do not handle stress well. You are often agitated and difficult to deal with.

What to Do

☑ *Take your pulse.* One useful barometer of how overwhelmed you are is to take your pulse during an argument. Usually a pulse over 85 beats per minute is an indication that your agitation is too high and your ability to think and act rationally is compromised. A pulse above 95 is absolutely too high. You will know you have calmed down sufficiently when your pulse returns to at or near normal, just over 70 beats per minute.

☑ *Breathe.* A simple and effective way to calm down is to do abdominal breathing. This can be done while listening to your partner speak or it can be done during a break from discussions. You need not breathe deeply. Take normal breaths. However, your abdomen should expand as you inhale. Place your hand on your abdomen while inhaling. Your hand should rise and fall. If your chest expands more than your abdomen you are not breathing properly and you may cause a subtle hyperventilation response. Breathing improperly can create uncomfortable sensations such as dizziness and tingling in the extremities.

It can take several minutes of proper breathing to calm you down sufficiently to be able to resume a difficult discussion. Allow time for that to occur. Impatience is not helpful.

☑ *Make repair statements.* Use the repair statements discussed in **Secret #22**. Repair statements have the effect of taking the pressure out of the conversation.

☑ *Think rationally.* Monitor your thoughts. Thoughts that include the following will only add to your agitation:

● *Thoughts of victimization.* Instead, can you think of how you have contributed to the problems?

● *Thoughts of righteous indignation.* Instead, can you think of any merit to your spouse's complaints? Are you the only one who is right? Is it possible to give your spouse the benefit of the doubt?

● *Character assassination.* Are you labeling your spouse in a heavy-handed way (he's lazy; she doesn't care; he's selfish; she can't be trusted, and so on)?

● *Thoughts that malign your spouse's intentions.* Might your spouse have done something wrong but with good intentions? Might your spouse have done something "mindlessly" and not maliciously?

☑ *Be honest.* List your complaints against your spouse and then, as honestly as you can, ask yourself if you are guilty of the same things. For example, if you accuse your spouse of not listening, do you always listen well? If your spouse is inconsiderate, do you ever act that way? Ask yourself if you hurt *yourself* in the same manner you accuse your spouse of hurting you. For example, if you say to your spouse "You never put me first," are you guilty of not meeting your needs? Do you always sacrifice for others at your expense? Perhaps if you treated yourself more fairly once in a while you'd be less focused on how your spouse treats you.

☑ *Sit, don't stand, during an argument.* It's usually not a good idea to stand up during an argument. That increases the odds of more agitation and premature exits. Try to remain seated.

Keep in Mind

♡ The most important times to calm down during an argument are as it starts to escalate or during a time-out.

♡ If your heart rate gets above 85 beats per minute during an argument it's time to de-escalate.

♡ Never pursue someone to complete the discussion if he or she is feeling overwhelmed.

♡ A few minutes of focused abdominal breathing will help relax you.

Keep It Between the Two of You

When the tension between two people rises to an uncomfortable level, an interesting phenomenon often occurs: A third person is drawn into the scene to distract the twosome from their conflict. That lowers the couple's anxiety but postpones any opportunity for the two to resolve the conflict by themselves. Sometimes the third person gets pulled into the two-person system, such as when a wife, frustrated with her husband, calls her mother to complain. Sometimes the third person enters voluntarily to rescue one of the two, serve as a referee to both, or simply divert attention away from the quarreling duo, such as when a young child spills her milk and distracts her arguing parents, or a father intervenes between a quarreling mother and son. When a duo becomes a trio in the manner just described, an *emotional triangle* has formed.

Emotional triangles are everywhere. Ever been to a party where many of the people don't know one another? Often they lower their anxiety by diverting their attention to something safe, like a beverage or a television program—"Excuse me,

I need a refill . . ." Being in a triangle is not a problem, but remaining in a triangle is. When a triangle forms, the basic problems between two people don't get resolved, they get reshelved—put on hold. A reshelved problem lowers anxiety in the short run but adds anxiety in the long run, as problems and issues accumulate like unopened bills.

Sometimes the third point in the emotional triangle is not a person: As Kyle became unhappier with Karen, he found ways to spend more time working; his job was the third point. Karen then had a new issue to complaint about, and Kyle tried to spend even *more* time away from home.

Clues to Hidden Triangles

Triangles operate freely because participants rarely know when they are in a triangle. Problematic children who interrupt quarreling parents don't make a conscious decision to intrude, and the quarreling parents don't make a conscious decision to argue within earshot of the over-involved child. Many people caught in the middle have noble intentions. They wish to ease another person's pain or help heal the troubled relationship. But on a subconscious level it is their own pain (the need to feel loved, competent, or in control) that drives them.

How can you tell whether you are trapped in an emotional triangle? The more common clues are:

● Finding yourself "in the middle" of a conflict between two other people. Or, seeking out a third person to help you lower your anxiety in your relationship with someone else.

- Feeling responsible for solving other people's problems.
- Gossip, or talking about a third person behind his back.
- The presence of a scapegoat or "black sheep." As long as there is someone else to blame for your misery, you never have to face yourself.
- Arguments or conflicts that never get resolved.

Disconnecting yourself from an emotional triangle isn't easy. Since the purpose of a triangle is to reduce anxiety, disconnecting yourself will serve to raise anxiety temporarily. Consequently, you'll be strongly tempted to rejoin the triangle and stabilize the situation.

Marge used to listen (unhappily) for hours while her mother complained to her about her "selfish and lazy" father. (Marge was the last child to leave home and felt guilty for doing so.) Finally she told her mother, "I feel bad that you are so unhappy. But from now on I think you should talk to Dad directly or perhaps see a counselor." Her mom acted hurt and angry, which made Marge feel guilty. She almost agreed to once again listen to her mom's complaints but was able to stand her ground, saying, "Mom, I'm going to hang up now." Her mom became angrier and didn't call back for two weeks. Instead she called Marge's brother and complained to him about Marge (another triangle). Fortunately, the brother was a psychologist who knew about emotional triangles. He knew it would be a mistake to agree with his mom that Marge was wrong, or to try to talk to Marge on his mom's behalf. Instead, he simply acknowledged to his mom that she seemed upset and wished her good luck in resolving her problem. That frustrated Mom but kept most of the anxiety where it should have been— between Mom and her husband, not in the laps of Marge or her brother.

What to Do

☑ *Identify the triangles in which you participate; otherwise, you can't unhook yourself.* In which relationships are you the "middleman"? Do you gossip or do others gossip to you, resulting in further alienation between you and someone else? When tension is high between you and another, how does that tension diminish? Does one of you get distracted by a third person ("It's time to help the kids with homework") or an event ("We can't talk now, it's time to go to bed")? Detecting triangles requires you to be a bit detached from the ordinary push and pull of a situation. If it's too difficult to notice your own triangles, begin by hunting for triangles that don't involve you. For example, have you overheard two coworkers complaining about a third? Watch your favorite television program (soap operas and situation comedies about families are perfect) and search for triangles there. Once you've identified a few, you may be more adept at identifying triangles of your own making.

☑ *To unhook yourself from a triangle where you are caught in the middle don't offer advice.* Unhooking yourself is a delicate operation. You must detach yourself from the emotional pressure to get involved but still remain connected to the other people. Running and hiding doesn't remove you from a triangle. It's your emotional involvement more than your physical presence that is required to keep a triangle in operation. Summarizing what the other person just said to you—"So you're telling me that you're lonely living with Dad"—is a way of staying connected without getting caught up in the problem. Never give advice; never take sides.

☑ *Repeat yourself.* If caught in the middle and reflective listening doesn't bring relief, be a broken record. Tell the complaining person to talk directly to the one being complained about, not to you. Say it over and over. If that doesn't help, you can exit the situation (by leaving or hanging up) but *do not leave in anger or frustration.* Better to say, "I know you're frustrated by your problem but I don't like being in the middle. I'm going to hang up now but I'll talk to you soon. Good luck." Remember, as long as you are emotionally charged, you can't unhook yourself from a triangle.

☑ *Do it on purpose.* Once you and your partner agree that triangles are a problem for you, purposely "triangle in" a third person during discussions with your spouse—then attempt to disconnect the triangle. Sometimes the best way to reduce automatic behavior patterns is to force yourself to do it more frequently. Doing so makes you much more aware of a process that ordinarily occurs automatically. Once that happens, you can change that process more easily than if you weren't aware.

☑ *Once you've successfully unhooked yourself from a triangle, answer this question:* What would have to happen for you to get re-involved in the same triangle? Once out of a triangle, there will be great pressure for you to return. Predicting ahead of time what the pressure will be and how you might resist it will improve the odds that you can stay out of problematic triangles. *Hint:* One useful way of resisting pressure is to inform the other person (before he tries to re-involve you in the triangle) what he'll probably say or do to try to re-involve you. Such a prediction reduces the other person's influence over you.

Keep in Mind

♡ People caught in the middle never receive the appreciation they feel they deserve and usually end up with most of the anxiety.

♡ If you must talk with someone else about your marital problem, commit to talking with your mate about the issue at least twice as long as you discuss it with someone else.

♡ If you must talk with someone else about your marital problem, tell your spouse everything you told the third person and tell the third person that everything being discussed will be told to your spouse. No exceptions.

♡ If you are feeling trapped in the middle, the only piece of advice you should offer is this: "I can't talk to you anymore about your problem. Talk to the person with whom you're having the problem."

Don't Tempt Fate with Opposite-Sex Friendships

Cara was married when she met a man at the cafeteria line at work. After a week of friendly glances she and the man sat next to each other during lunch and had a pleasant conversation. It wasn't long before Cara started looking forward to her lunches with Jack. And of course, it was innocent—after all, they were only having lunch in a public place at work. Soon they learned more about each other's lives. Neither one was unhappy in their marriage but each made a point of suggesting that their marriage wasn't as exciting and passionate as it could be.

Three months later the lunches turned into meetings after work for a cup of coffee. Or they somehow "ran into each other" at the mall. E-mails became almost daily rituals, as did calls to each other on their cell phones.

Cara never told her husband about Jack. And she'd make secret calls to Jack at night when her husband went to bed. Still, she and Jack never kissed or had any sexual contact. It was those two facts that kept Cara thinking her relationship was Jack was above-board, innocent, and "just friends." The truth is that Cara had begun an "emotional affair" and refused to admit it. And she was perilously close to having a sexual affair. But couldn't she have opposite-sex friendships? Can't married men and women have close, caring friendships with members of the opposite sex?

Affairs of the Heart

Which of the following statements do you think is, for the most part, true?

A married person who has an affair must be very unhappy in the marriage. Actually, happy people can still fall in love or be tempted to have an affair if the right person and opportunities present themselves. Many people who have affairs did not intend to have them.

A person who has an affair probably has a weak character. Yes, there are cads and serial adulterers. But many people who have affairs are not bad people, but lonely people.

Affairs that are "just about sex" are less damaging to a marriage than affairs that involve deeper feelings. Dishonesty and lack of trust are most damaging to a marriage. The sexual aspect of an affair, while painful to a betrayed spouse, is not as agonizing as the inability to regain the feeling of and being the recipient of trust.

A person who leaves a marriage to be with a lover will probably end up in a happier relationship. Statistically, only about 10 percent of adulterers end up with each other. And divorce is more likely the second time around.

Most marriages cannot recover from an affair. Some affairs happen at the end of an already dying relationship. But when a couple wants to reconcile, it is very possible to achieve that.

How to Tell When Your Friendships Are Tempting Fate

Opposite-sex friendships can be healthy and normal but some opposite-sex friends are playing with fire. When opposite-sex friends (OSFs) truly are "just friends" their friendship does not interfere in any way with their marriages. For example, if you spend time socializing with your OSF *at the expense of time with your spouse* then your friendship must be looked at more closely. Are you running from your spouse? Or are you really running *toward* your OSF?

Good friends will talk and spend time with one another. But if they are innocent friendships there will be no secretiveness. In fact, it's more likely that spouses will all participate in getting together.

The real ingredient to watch for is *attraction*. Are you physically attracted to your OSF? Do you "have feelings"? Do you fantasize about that person? Now you are swimming in more dangerous waters. First, there is nothing wrong per se about being attracted to or even having a deep affection for someone other than your spouse. The world is full of people with beautiful looks and beautiful spirits who will catch your eye

? Did You Know?

Online sexual connections via chat rooms are more prominent these days. Many people consider them to be innocent because they are not meeting with the online partner. Instead, they view it as fun—similar to playing a video game. However, online sex via chat rooms or instant messaging is a form of cheating. If your partner tells you it is innocent or "everybody does it" don't believe it. Online sex damages marriages.

and possibly your heart. But if you are emotionally attracted to an OSF you run a risk of walking down a slippery slope of extramarital involvement. You have to reverse direction. It's not how you feel so much as it is what you do with your feelings that will make the difference.

So, friendship plus physical/emotional attraction is a one–two combination you need to pay attention to. A final ingredient is *opportunity*. The more opportunity to have time with your OSF, especially private time (meetings, e-mails, phone calls), the greater the chance you will develop an emotional or a physical affair. Of course, many people can resist the temptations. You're better off limiting your involvement if the three variables of friendship-attraction–opportunity exist. You only need to slip up one time to make your life and the lives of your family a mess.

You don't necessarily have to end your friendship if you have a physical attraction to the OSF. But you must take steps to put up more walls between you and the OSF *and at the same time* take steps to break down any walls between you and your spouse. One step without the other will be futile.

What to Do

☑ *Reduce opportunities.* If you are sexually attracted to an OSF you must limit your time together (both in person and in electronic communications) and you must alter the nature of your communications so that there are no more secrets. In other words, contact each other significantly less often and when you do contact each other let your spouse know the details.

☑ *Eliminate flirting of any kind.* There are some people you might be friends with and are sexually attracted to and yet you know without question that the OSF is unavailable romantically. He or she gives off a strong signal to that effect. Typically, that person doesn't flirt or make any comments that can be construed as a "come-on." Be that kind of person. Otherwise you will send signals you will deny sending (but in your heart you'll know you did).

☑ *Reduce your fantasies.* It's hard to eliminate all fantasies of someone you are attracted to. However, you should not deliberately nurture such fantasies. Often, when a marriage is in rocky shape, a person might engage in many fantasies about an OSF and actively avoid their mate in the process. Better to start focusing on the qualities of the spouse you love or admire and think of ways to connect more strongly to your spouse.

☑ *Emphasize the nonromantic qualities of your OSF—including his or her faults.* Focus on why he or she is a good friend but keep from putting him or her on a pedestal. What unflattering qualities does your OSF possess?

☑ *Imagine the negative consequences of an affair.* The consequences of an affair are rarely pretty. Yes there is passion and drama and the rush that comes with infatuation or falling in love. But there is anxiety, fear of being found out, the need to keep lying, and the pain to families if an affair is exposed. If an affair happens in part because a marriage is less than satisfying, continuing the affair will prevent the marriage from improving since there will be no motivation to make changes.

☑ *Jump-start your marriage love life.* Go on a romantic getaway. Buy gifts. Show more passion and excitement. Find ways to compliment your spouse. Have more date nights. Purposely devote much more energy to your spouse.

Keep in Mind

♡ Opposite-sex friendships can be wonderful and life enhancing, but any romantic feelings must not be allowed to flourish.

♡ A deep affection for an OSF is possible without it being a threat to a marriage. But be careful.

♡ If you definitely have a strong physical attraction to an OSF you need to reduce your time together and spend time enhancing your marriage. Otherwise, complications can result.

♡ It's normal to have sexual fantasies about others. It's dangerous to purposely nurture those fantasies at the expense of your marriage.

♡ Happy, mature spouses aren't jealous; neither do happy spouses give one another reason to feel jealous.

Secret #26

Abandon Resentment, and Forgive

To genuinely forgive after suffering a deep hurt or loss is one of the hardest things you will ever do. Some people forgive quickly, not out of sincere love and understanding but out of fear. Motivated to avoid rejection, to gain approval, or to appease, they forgive for the wrong reasons and never feel completely free. Some withhold forgiveness until they get to the bottom of what happened. Betrayed spouses often ask themselves question after endless question in an attempt to discover the "truth": *Does he really love me? Would he ever betray me again? What was his real reason for betraying me?* Never knowing for sure when they've discovered the truth, they can't free themselves to forgive.

For a couple to be truly happy, forgiveness is not an option. It's a necessity. While it's possible to forgive a person but not stay in a relationship with them, it's not possible to truly reconcile without forgiveness.

What Forgiveness Is and Isn't

What is forgiveness? Dr. Robert Enright at the University of Wisconsin is a leading researcher on forgiveness. He defines it as a willingness to abandon resentment and negative judgment toward the offender (and the injured person has a right to the negative judgment) while fostering some sort of goodwill or compassion toward the offender (who does not deserve it). Some people confuse forgiveness with forgetting. Forgetting is not a sign of forgiveness. The deeper the hurt, the longer you will remember it. But when you forgive and feel free to resume trusting, more of your time is spent doing positive things and your mind is no longer preoccupied with the hurt.

Some feel that to forgive is to somehow minimize the wrongdoing. That isn't so. The wrongdoing must be clearly recognized for what it is before forgiveness, if it is desired, can be applied. Forgiveness is not a quick fix, either. It can take time to forgive and the hurtful partner must endeavor to not be hurtful in that way again.

Some withhold forgiveness, not merely out of vengeance but as a way to exercise control over a relationship that got out of control. "I was made a fool. I'll be damned if I let her hurt me that way again." This is an understandable sentiment but one that, if maintained, becomes self-defeating.

The challenges of forgiveness are many. For example, Marian said, "I've tried to forgive, I really have. But each day when I wake up the feeling isn't there. How can I forgive him when I don't *feel* forgiving?" A common mistake made by well-intentioned people is to believe they must feel forgiving before they can finally forgive. While it is not helpful to pretend you are no longer hurt and angry when you are, forgiveness begins as a decision, not as a feeling. You must first choose to forgive before you can ever feel forgiving.

Forgiveness is also a challenge because there is a tendency to quickly forget what was right about a relationship after we have been wronged. One woman, after she learned that her husband had had a brief affair two years earlier, totally revised her view of him. "I couldn't help myself," she explained. "I'd remember all the times he went out of his way to do something nice for me. I used to think he was wonderful for doing those things. Now I think he did it to trick me, to keep me off his trail. Maybe he was considerate because he felt guilty; I'm not sure. All I know is that I'm questioning everything he did for me. Everything." In fact, her relationship had brought her years of joy—all of which, sadly, had become suspect.

"I'm Sorry, But . . ."

It's amazing how many partners never apologize for their hurtful actions. Sometimes they blame their behavior on their spouse, claiming, "You made me do it." Sometimes they do apologize and add, "But you must understand that I was under a lot of pressure at the time." Saying "I'm sorry, but—" rarely feels like a sincere apology. These halfhearted apologies are understandable, however. Often, the person is trying to *explain* his or her actions, but the explanation is misinterpreted as an attempt to *justify* the actions. Sometimes the betrayed person unwittingly puts the explaining spouse in a double bind. For example:

> *"Why did you hurt me like that?"*
>
> *"I don't know."*
>
> *"You don't know? How can I ever learn to trust you if you say you don't know? Surely you must know something?"*
>
> *"Maybe I hurt you because I was angry at you for being so controlling and demanding. I'm not your possession."*
>
> *"Oh, so you're telling me it's my fault you flirted with your boss?"*

In this case, the husband's attempt to know why his wife acted flirtatiously prompted her to give an explanation that sounded self-serving. But having no explanation was not acceptable to him, either.

Bringing Up the Past

Efforts to forgive get sidetracked when one partner focuses on past injustices while the other wants to focus only on current problems. While most self-help books advise against rewashing old laundry, diversions to the past usually happen for good reasons. Rather than make a blanket rule disallowing any excursions into the past, it is best to inquire (sincerely, not sarcastically) why it is important for a spouse to bring up old issues. For example, when you believe your mate is downplaying his offense, you may be bringing up past issues as a way to impress upon your partner the extent of your pain. Simply accusing— "Why must you keep bringing up *that* old issue?"—may add insult to injury and further complicate the forgiveness process. If the issue of bringing up the past continues to sidetrack your efforts at forgiveness, take turns having discussions where the past is allowed and disallowed as a topic.

Phases of Forgiveness

Researchers believe that people tend to go through four phases before they can forgive a deep hurt. Not everyone needs to go through each phase in order to experience forgiveness, and some people must repeat certain phases, but for the most part they represent the typical steps taken in forgiveness and reconciliation.

Phase One: Uncovering

This phase involves trying to understand the full nature and extent of the hurt. This can be a complicated phase because of our tendency to either deny certain truths or to imagine things that aren't true. At this phase the injured party is obsessed with thoughts such as "Why did this happen? How could he do that to me? Will I ever get over it?" At this phase, ask yourself if you feel mostly a loss of love or a loss of esteem or a loss of control. Once you know where the primary injury lies, you can take steps to heal. For example, if a partner hurts you and it affects mostly your self-esteem, you now know that you need to build your self-esteem in whatever ways you can. You might want to improve your appearance or find a more challenging job or learn a new skill. Distorting the truth complicates forgiveness. If you pretend you weren't really hurt when in fact you were, you won't see the need to forgive. But you will harbor anxiety and never feel fully content with the relationship. If you can acknowledge the hurt, you must then examine it more closely. Were you hurt like that before? By whom? How did you handle it then? At Phase One, the hurtful person needs to own up to being hurtful and examine what caused it.

Phase Two: Decision

At this phase the notion of forgiveness becomes a possibility. Here people realize that their anger simply isn't going away and that something else must happen. They might struggle with forgiveness, believing that it somehow lets the offending party off the hook. But eventually they see forgiveness as the only path to take. Here a person might say, "I want to forgive but I can't . . . Forgiveness doesn't seem fair . . . I don't know how to forgive." Here the realization starts to take hold that forgiveness is more of a decision than a feeling. One must act forgiving before one can ever feel forgiving.

Phase Three: Work

Have a dialogue with your partner for the purpose of gaining understanding. The dialogue should not be an inquisition. No one should be an interrogator ready to pass judgment. The goal is to discover what led up to the hurtful actions. Even if you were the one betrayed, examining your role in the relationship is vital at this phase. You did not cause your partner's infidelity, for example, but you may have been contributing to the unhappiness in the marriage. Remember, the dialogue to understanding is necessarily limited. It is difficult to ascertain all the reasons why things happened the way they did.

The work phase involves efforts to better understand the offender and develop some degree of compassion for him or her. It's a time when the good qualities of the offender come to the forefront of your mind, not just the negative qualities. In this phase the offended person must realize that the pain must be absorbed. In other words, lashing out with vengeance is not the answer. There can be no payback that will truly make amends.

Phase Four: Deepening

Here love and trust grow and anger withers. It's also a time when a deeper meaning to what happened might be discerned. For example, you might conclude that what happened made you somehow a better person despite the pain. You might regard your relationship as stronger in some ways. Or you may have learned something very important about your relationship or about life.

Remnant feelings of anger and guilt may arise from time to time. That does not necessarily mean you haven't been fully forgiving or forgiven. Reminding yourself of the good aspect of both your mate and of your relationship can help steer you away from pain and toward contentment. Sometimes what you must let go of are longstanding myths. Maybe you believed your mate would be all perfect. Maybe you believed that love meant never having to say you're sorry. Regardless, leaving behind what you have outgrown is required of a healthy, satisfying life.

If you have ever forgiven someone, or been forgiven, then you know how possible true forgiveness is. But it does require effort, patience, and commitment. When you wish to forgive (yourself or someone else), some additional guidelines can help.

What to Do

☑ *Allow an unimpeded opportunity to express pain.* For three days during the week (more or less, if needed) set aside ten to twenty minutes to recite your list of grievances. Your partner is to listen, summarizing so as to convey he heard you, but not to challenge or debate you. After the third day your partner is to write a letter of apology for the hurts against you and for his role in the weakening of the marriage. He should admit guilt when he is guilty and ask for forgiveness. Then do the exercise again, this time reversing roles. As uncomfortable as this might be, it allows you to clear the air and express yourself in an unimpeded manner. And it provides the opportunity for a well-thought-out apology.

☑ *Act forgiving, even if you don't feel forgiving.* How would you be acting today (or during the next hour) if you had forgiven your mate? Act accordingly. You are not denying your pain in this exercise but helping to move past your anger and toward reconciliation. If you wait to feel forgiving before you act forgiving, you may have to wait a much longer time than you deserve.

☑ *Do the "I forgive you" task.* I discussed this task in my book, *The Forgiving Marriage: Overcoming Anger and Resentment and Rediscovering Each Other* and it can reveal feelings you didn't even know you had. Imagine the other person is seated directly across from you. Repeat aloud the words "I forgive you" and notice the thoughts that follow. Did you think "But I'm still angry" or "You don't deserve forgiveness"? Repeat the phrase "I forgive you" and again notice your thoughts. Doing this about ten times results in one of two outcomes: either no thoughts follow the phrase and you simply feel more forgiving, or one thought continues to recur. In the latter case, the recurring thought represents some unresolved issue for you. Recognizing that allows you the opportunity to examine that issue closely or talk it over with your mate. The "I forgive you" exercise helps you either way.

☑ *If you've been forgiven but your mate still mentions the hurt against him, don't criticize.* Resentment and anger doesn't vanish immediately after forgiveness, despite best intentions. And some places or situations—a certain restaurant, day of the week, etc.—may remind your mate of what you did that was hurtful. Understand that he still needs to talk about it from time to time, and understand that his mood may fluctuate. Don't take it personally and don't condemn him for his feelings. Say instead, "I don't blame you for having those feelings. I wish you didn't have to feel that way, but I understand it's not easy to forget." That demonstrates compassion and understanding and probably will hasten his recovery.

☑ *Meditate or pray.* Finding an inner calmness or peace can help you gain perspective. Try to discern if some greater good can be achieved by forgiving.

☑ *Perform a ritual together to symbolize your renewal in your marriage.* Plant a tree or garden in honor of your future together. Renew your marriage vows. Buy a wedding cake. Give your partner a small gift or piece of jewelry—something to symbolize your reconciliation and love for one another. Such a ritual helps put emotional closure on some bad feelings and is a nice way to begin a new future together.

Keep in Mind

♡ "I forgive you" is as important a phrase as "I love you."

♡ If you still feel resentful, you feel owed. What are you owed? If you still feel guilty, you feel you owe. What do you owe?

♡ Forgiveness begins as a decision, not a feeling.

♡ Apologies can soothe but they do not heal. Apologies should be sincere, not said in an offhand way.

♡ Whoever hurt you did so not because you were unlovable but because he or she had weaknesses.

Secret #27

Don't Keep Bringing Up the Past

Do these phrases sound familiar?

> *"I thought we were over that?"*
> *"Can't you forgive and forget?"*
> *"Why must you always bring that up?"*
> *"Stop throwing it in my face."*

If they do, then you and your spouse have had the occasional argument punctuated by reminders of past mistakes. It isn't fatal when it happens but rarely does it help move the conversation along. Instead, the discussion derails into a debate about why old mistakes must be resurrected.

Actually, even though bringing up the past isn't all that helpful, often there are valid reasons why the past is being mentioned. If a couple can figure out why the past keeps coming up, the need to have it keep coming up will diminish.

Listening Helps

Good listening involves hearing more than just the words. It means being able to sort through what's being said and detect a *leading-edge feeling*. A leading-edge feeling is the main feeling a speaker wants to be understood and accepted. For example, hearing the complaint "You're always late!" might make you want to respond, "I'm not *always* late." True, you're probably right when you make that fine distinction. But the point is not that you are late or even always late. The point is that your partner is angry, frustrated, and possibly hurt (all leading-edge feelings) that *once again* you are late.

By hearing the words but ignoring your partner's leading-edge feeling you will not have a satisfying discussion. Similarly, if a partner throws the past in your face, look to see if you can detect a leading-edge feeling and ignore the fact that the past was brought up. Is your partner frustrated? Is that why she reminded you of past mistakes? Better then to discuss her frustration.

What to Do

☑ *View bringing up the past as a clue to an underlying concern.* Then address the concern instead of complaining that the past was being dragged up. For example, if your spouse brings up past mistakes you might say, "I notice you're bringing up the past again. Is it still bothering you? Does it feel like I haven't been listening?"

☑ *Ask, "What is it you want me to understand that you don't think I understand?"* This will help your partner clarify what her main issues are.

☑ *Don't shut down the conversation.* If you need a time-out from a tense discussion (see **Secret #23**) that's fine. But stonewalling and refusing to discuss matters because you are annoyed that the past was dragged up will not get you what you ultimately want. Better to try to deal squarely with the issues being presented.

☑ *If you're criticized for bringing up the past, don't get defensive.* Acknowledge that your partner has a right to feel frustrated. But point out that you're reason for bringing up the past is not to batter the person with it but to get across a point. Then state what that point is. Say, "Please bear with me" if your spouse is aggravated.

❓ Did You Know?

It can be a great thing to bring up *positive* reminders of the past. Reminiscing can add to a sense of closeness as warm memories are shared. Nostalgia is wonderful. While some people can go overboard and seem to live only in the glorious past and miss out on today, a more common occurrence is for one partner to warmly say "Oh, remember the time when . . . " and the other to barely give lip service to the discussion. If your partner likes to reminisce, take a few minutes to respond positively to what's being said and share in the memory. Make it a nice moment for the two of you.

Keep in Mind

♡ Even happy couples will bring up old mistakes from time to time. But keep it to a minimum.

♡ Figure out why the past is being brought up instead of getting angry that it's happening.

♡ When in doubt or at an impasse on what to do, yield to your partner's wishes.

Reduce Conversation Killers

"You know what would be really enjoyable?" Pam said excitedly to her husband, Mark.

"Tell me," he answered slyly, eager to please.

"Since both of us don't go to work on Thursday mornings, wouldn't it be great if around 9:00 A.M. we sat down, poured ourselves some coffee, and just talked for an hour? Mark? Honey, can you hear me? Mark, your eyes have glazed over again . . ."

On average, wives enjoy talking with their mates more than husbands do. To women, the essence of any friendship is the ability to talk freely and disclose deep feelings. Men, however, rarely discuss their innermost feelings with their friends—wives included. Intimacy in male friendships shows up as good-natured teasing and "doing things together," such as playing racquetball or watching a ball game. Consequently, after an evening of television viewing with their wives, many husbands are surprised to hear their wives complain, "We don't do anything together anymore."

Happy couples aren't dynamic conversationalists. Neither do they have dialogues without occasional misunderstandings and slip-ups. But most of the time their conversations have a flow—a constructive, mostly smooth, back-and-forth exchange of ideas. When things get heated or complicated, happy couples know how to de-escalate and calm down (**Secrets #22** and **23**). Communication is a key skill for couples because talking is the main tool available to deal with differences. When talking skills are poor, it's like trying to build a house with inadequate tools—good luck.

What Goes Wrong?

How do efforts to have a simple dialogue get bogged down? There are three possible reasons:

1. *Conflicting expectations.* According to author Deborah Tannen, being able to talk things out is a sign to most women that the relationship is working. But to men, the relationship is not working well if you have to keep talking about it. The key is expectations. As long as couples who rarely talk beyond superficial matters never expect more than that, they will be satisfied.

2. *The mechanics of conversation.* For effective dialogue, the speaker must first say what he means. "I'm upset" is vague. It can mean anything from "I'm annoyed" to "I'm furious." "Let's go out for dinner tonight" might imply "You arrange for a babysitter and I'll make the

dinner reservations." Do you know what your mate means when she says, "I'm tired"? Is she stating a fact or is she making a request for you to watch the kids for a while?

If a speaker successfully says what he means, does the listener hear the message accurately? When Ken said, "Let's go to a movie this weekend," Sarah was annoyed. She heard Ken's remark as a *demand* ("We are going to the movies") when in fact he expressed a desire and was quite willing to negotiate. Conversations also get complicated when nonverbal expressions (e.g., a bored look) don't match the spoken words ("I'm having a great time at this party"). As a general rule, when there is an inconsistency between verbal and nonverbal expressions, people view the nonverbal signs as a true reflection of how someone is feeling. Unfortunately, men are better at decoding the nonverbal messages of strangers than those of their wives. And men's decoding skills worsen when their wives are distressed. It appears that a husband's anxiety increases

? Did You Know . . .

Interrupting a partner is not such a conversational blunder after all. In one study, happy couples interrupted one another almost twice as much as unhappy couples. The real issue is how an interruption is interpreted. Happy couples view interruptions as signs of interest by their partners. Unhappy couples view an interruption as rude. Similarly, "mind reading" (telling a spouse what's on his or her mind) is viewed by happy couples as a gentle "feeling probe" while unhappy couples see it as intrusive. The point is that happy couples will find positive explanations for actions that unhappy partners will object to.

when his wife is unhappy, and his anxiety impairs his ability to understand her nonverbal messages.

3. *The environment.* Trying to talk effectively when the kids are raising a ruckus, the radio is blaring, or when you are about to leave for work increases the chances for miscommunication. Reducing distractions is necessary, especially for important discussions.

Conversation Killers

There is no question that hostile verbal attacks or emotional shutdowns wreak havoc on conversations and the relationship as a whole. But there are numerous, more subtle mistakes couples make when conversing. In fact, partners don't often recognize when they are making these blunders.

- *Hasty reassurances.* Statements like "I'm sure you'll do fine . . . Don't worry about it . . . Everything will turn out fine" and so forth, may sound reasonable but can come off as dismissive. It looks as if you are trying to get the conversation over with.
- *Minimizing the other's feelings.* Similar to giving hasty reassurances, you minimize a partner's feelings when you convey the idea that he or she is wrong to feel a certain way. "Don't be so upset . . . I can't believe you're getting so angry . . . You're making a big deal out of things . . . You're too emotional." Your partner may in fact be overreacting. However, it's better to ask questions ("Why do you feel

that way?") than to automatically judge the other's feelings as unnecessary or wrong.

- *Speaking in clichés.* "That's life . . . No one ever expected it to be easy . . . You have to break a few eggs . . . " Clichés might be appropriate but then again they might indicate a casual attitude on the part of the listener. The speaker may not feel fully understood or listened to. If you respond with a cliché and your partner sounds a bit more edgy or frustrated, you probably blundered.

- *Parental comments.* Anything you say that comes off as a scolding or conveys the idea that you "know best" will not be appreciated. It shows a lack of respect for the other's opinions. If your partner feels talked down to, you're coming off as a parent.

- *Childish comments.* Do you whine? Do you have temper tantrums or figuratively stomp your feet when you don't get your way? Do you pout? Ask yourself how emotionally old you feel at such times. If your answer is below age twenty-one you're definitely not acting as maturely as you could.

- *Making "Hurry up!" comments or gestures.* Trying to get your partner to speed through his or her comments conveys impatience. Maybe you're partner is talking too long or not getting to the point. But acting impatient won't help. An honest and respectful way to respond might be, "Can you tell me what your main concern is first and then you can fill in all the details? You're saying quite a lot. Can we take your points one at a time?"

- *Hearing the words but not understanding the spirit of the message.* Don't nitpick about details you disagree with and overlook the main concerns your partner might have. For example, if your spouse complains that you are often inattentive, replying "I'm not *always* inattentive" or "I wasn't *that* inattentive" misses the point. Don't get bogged down on the fine points of a disagreement.

- *"That reminds me of the time . . . "* When a spouse is revealing their feelings or some important bit of information, don't get sidetracked by telling your own personal stories. At that moment you are really communicating, "What you're saying isn't that important. Listen to me instead."

- *Silence.* Researchers say that "pitching back" by at least making comments such as "Uh huh . . . Interesting . . . Tell me more . . . Hmmm . . . Wow . . . " and so on indicate that you are really listening. Nonverbal indicators are important, too, such as eye contact or a gentle touch.

What to Do

☑ *Validate a partner's comments.* Comments are validated not when you agree with them but when you can say, "Given your perception of events, your ideas on what to do make sense," or "Given your interpretations, I don't blame you for feeling the way you do." Most people believe their reactions make perfect sense. Having a different point of view is not divisive. Expressing it in a manner that conveys, "You are foolish to feel the way you do," is. If you can't validate your partner's comments, then you don't fully understand them.

☑ *Don't offer advice or solutions to problems unless explicitly asked* (husbands, especially, take heed). There are two kinds of communication: expression of one's feelings and thoughts, and problem solving. Often, one partner's wish to blow off steam—to express feelings about a hard day—is interpreted by the other as an invitation to problem solve. Husbands in particular have a difficult time listening to their wives discuss personal problems without trying to solve the problems. Many wives resent that. This pattern also occurs when one partner simply expresses a wish and the other responds to it as if it were a topic for negotiation (a problem to be solved):

> *"Wouldn't it be great if we had a boat?"*
>
> *"A boat? You know we can't afford a boat."*
>
> *"I wasn't saying we should buy one, I was just saying it would be nice if we had one."*
>
> *"No use talking about something we won't get."*

Learn to recognize which kind of communication is needed (expression of feelings or problem-solving), and you won't miss the boat when it comes to constructive dialogue.

☑ *Write two letters to clear up confusion and improve mutual understanding*: a letter to your partner stating your point of view and a letter to yourself stating your partner's point of view. This exercise was inspired by research discussed by Howard Markman and can be very helpful, as a thoughtful, sincere letter can halt uncooperative dialogues and convey understanding better than some verbal exchanges. Eventually, successful letter writing leads to successful verbal dialogue, since each partner is now more willing to listen and give his or her mate the benefit of the doubt.

Keep In Mind

♡ Even happy couples mess up conversations now and then. But they endeavor to correct mistakes when they can.

♡ Expect complications and misunderstandings if your nonverbal messages clash with your verbal messages.

♡ When discussions go nowhere, one or both of you is missing something important. Aim for mutual understanding, not winning the argument or being right.

♡ Taking an "I know best" attitude about issues comes off as parental and is a turnoff to most spouses. Relationships that are more parent/child or dominant/submissive are rarely satisfying.

Secret #29

Eliminate Double Standards

When Stan arrived home from work he wanted to go directly to the garage and finish up a project. His wife, Lydia, wanted him to look after the kids so she could run to the mall. Stan hemmed and hawed and blamed Lydia for not alerting him ahead of time that she might need him to babysit. But when she complained that he never forewarned her that he wanted to work in the garage he told her she should have simply assumed that. Stan often argued with that kind of logic. If he was upset about something and wanted to complain, Lydia was wrong not to listen. But if she was upset and wanted to complain, she was wrong for "bitching." Stan operated with double standards. Double standards are not fair and unfairness wreaks havoc in relationships.

Unwritten Rules

Double standards are rarely consciously agreed-upon rules. They are usually discovered or pointed out by a partner who feels unfairly treated. If a partner operates with a double standard that is advantageous to him or her, one of two things is happening: That double standard is mindless, and once pointed out, it will be corrected; or the double standard is used as a method of control, and once pointed out, will be hotly dismissed or criticized. If a partner refuses to acknowledge he is operating under a double standard or refuses to change it, the marriage will never be fully satisfying.

Double standards can exist about any topic or issue. More common ones include:

- One partner can spend money as he or she pleases while the other must get permission.
- One can take up hobbies that interfere with home life but the other cannot.
- One can have friends of the opposite sex but the other cannot without being challenged or interrogated.
- One's complaints or criticisms are always justifiable while the other's are unjustified.
- Saying no to sex is okay for one person but not the other.

In the worst cases, double standards indicate a controlling, possessive, insecure, or jealous partner. In many cases, double standards are simply unwritten rules of engagement that have evolved, without much scrutiny, over time. For example, despite the fact that most mothers today are in the work force, mothers still take on more of the child-rearing and housekeeping chores than their husbands. Consequently, many men still think of looking after their own children as baby-sitting, as if it's a tacked-on responsibility that isn't really theirs to bear. (Why is it that the phrase "mothering a child" means to nurture, while the phrase "fathering a child" means to get a woman pregnant?) Thus, in many families, the double standard is that if a mother wants to go out without the kids she needs to arrange it with her husband. If he wants to go out without the kids he just goes.

What to Do

☑ *Be honest.* If a double standard rears its ugly head, admit it and change it, don't defend it. Double standards are corrosive over time.

☑ *Don't passively submit.* Double standards persist because they serve one spouse's purpose and the other simply acquiesces. Yes, refusing to tolerate a double standard might cause problems and conflict in the short run. But in the long run the relationship benefits when they are reduced or eliminated.

☑ *Realize that the scales always balance eventually.* If one spouse gets his or her way unfairly on some issues, over time the other will compensate by being more distant or uncooperative in other areas. For example, it's not unusual that if a man controls the money in a relationship, the wife controls the sex. Fairness creates goodwill and cooperativeness.

Keep in Mind

♡ Double standards double the odds your marriage will be unhappy.

♡ Many double standards develop mindlessly, not out of malice but out of ignorance.

♡ Things can be fair without being equal. Husbands and wives might take on different responsibilities or one might be more "in charge" of some area than the other. But if such differences are agreed upon and not resented, such inequities are not unfair.

♡ Double standards reduce overall level of trust.

Get Rid of These Sexual Myths

Mark and Nancy had been married about two years when Nancy got a call from an old boyfriend. He wasn't interested in dating her again but he was depressed about a current break-up and wanted to chat with Nancy. He and Nancy had ended their relationship very pleasantly about five years earlier and while they'd rarely spoken since then, they still thought of themselves as friends. When Mark heard about it he got concerned. Why was that guy *really* calling, he wondered. Did Nancy still love him? Nancy admitted that she'd always have a warm spot in her heart for her ex but that she truly loved her husband and wanted only him. Mark wasn't so sure. "You can't love me and have love for someone else at the same time," he said. "If you really loved me . . . "

Mark thinks that true love means it would be impossible to have feelings for someone else. He is wrong. He's also insecure. The real test is not how Nancy feels but what she does with her feelings. That's just one example of how people who are otherwise bright and mature can get caught up in misguided beliefs that complicate their relationships.

The Naked Truth

Some of the biggest and most enduring misconceptions are about sex. Happy couples strip away false beliefs and see things more clearly. How many of these sexual myths do you believe?

☑ *Foreplay is essentially about physical stimulation so that the man gets an erection and the woman becomes lubricated.* People who believe this will ultimately have a boring sex life at best and most likely an infrequent sex life. Foreplay is not just a means to an end (intercourse) but is an end in itself. It's an opportunity to enjoy one another, like taking your time with a sumptuous meal. If you rush through foreplay you will miss some of the most pleasurable aspects of sex. Furthermore, foreplay can start hours and even days before you take your clothes off. It's often about attitude and how you treat one another when sex isn't in the immediate future. I often tell husbands that helping out more around the house (or doing anything that their wives would very much appreciate) is really a form of foreplay to a beleaguered wife and mother. Foreplay is thoughtfulness, tenderness, and devotion. And if you want great sex on a Friday night, foreplay starts by Friday morning at the latest—and often it needs to have started two days earlier.

☑ *Men who push for sex are "only interested in one thing."* If you're married and your husband keeps pushing for sex or seems displeased at the frequency of sex, he is really after love and connection, not merely an orgasm. The problem is that many men use sex as their main pathway to intimacy and allow the other pathways (especially conversation and self-disclosure) to atrophy. This sets up a pattern where the only way many men can feel close to their spouses is through sex. However, the woman—feeling neglected because her intimacy needs are not met just through sexual intimacy—withdraws from sex. That makes the man feel even more desirous of a sexual connection and he goes after it, often with less romance and tenderness. If you are a woman and you think your husband is only after one thing, he probably is: you.

☑ *Women are ready to make love when they are lubricated.* True, lubrication makes a woman ready for intercourse. But making love is something different. This goes back to the issue of foreplay and to the notion that women want to feel cherished in their marriage. When they do, they aren't just having sex—they are making love.

☑ *It's a problem if a man loses his erection during sex.* Not necessarily. While medical reasons (such as diabetes) exist for why a man might lose an erection, it is not unusual for a perfectly healthy man's penis to get flaccid during foreplay. That is especially true if the foreplay goes on for a long period of time and is not always genitally focused. That is not an automatic sign of old age or loss of potency. It is typically a sign of comfort and familiarity and (sometimes) lack of novelty. If you make a big deal over losing an erection, then it becomes a problem when it needn't be. If erection loss continues or becomes a source of chronic anxiety or leads to avoidance of sex, consult a physician or a qualified sex therapist.

☑ *Sexual fantasies about people other than your spouse indicate a problem.* More than 90 percent of people have regular sexual fantasies, and sometimes those fantasies are not about their partner. The fantasies in themselves are normal. However, obsessive preoccupation with sexual fantasies (as when someone regularly goes online to view pornography or engage in sexual chats with strangers) is a significant problem. Fantasizing about others is fine if it is innocent fun and if it eventually draws you to your spouse. Fantasizing that draws you away from your spouse emotionally or physically indicates a problem.

☑ *"Most people have a more interesting and passionate sex life than I do."* The truth is the average American's sex life is, well, average. That means it is nice, pleasant, somewhat stimulating, occasionally mundane, and occasionally fantastic. About a third of all people report occasional disinterest in sex. An average sex life doesn't mean that you shouldn't bother to upgrade your sexual megahertz. Happy couples get sexually adventurous and find creative ways to make love despite years together. It's less about technique (although any book on technique can be worth the investment to an inhibited couple) than it's about having fun with each other and cultivating an adventurous spirit.

☑ *If the sex is good, the rest of the relationship is good, too.* Most unhappy couples don't have a fantastic sex life. But many couples report they are quite content with their sex life but discontent with other areas. Don't let a good sex life fool you. Problems may be lurking. Men are particularly good at putting their heads in the sand and assuming that if they are having sex at least somewhat regularly their wives can't be all that unhappy. It isn't always true. Many people simply go along with sex at times when they aren't feeling that close to their partner. Look for other clues to assess the state of your relationship: Do you converse regularly in a meaningful way? Do you enjoy your time together and really look forward to each other's company? Are arguments kept to a minimum? Are there regular thought-ful gestures? Do you make love more often than you argue?

☑ *Quality is more important than quantity.* Actually, the two fac-tors are related. If quality is high and you are able to have mind-blowing sex, it's unlikely you will do it infrequently. And if you are having sex infrequently, it's probably not all fireworks and acrobatics when you do. Of course there is a limit to how often any couple can have sex depending upon factors such as fatigue, opportunity, and day-to-day responsibilities. But if you keep shouting the mantra that quality is better than quantity you are probably feeling guilty that you're not having enough sex. If you and your spouse have different desires when it comes to fre-quency of sex, but the quality of your sex life is good or better than good when you do have it, then your differences in desire are not making a difference in quality. That's a good sign.

What to Do

☑ *Stop letting popular media stereotypes dictate your views on sex.* If you only went by today's movies, TV shows, or women's maga-zines, your sex life would definitely seem inferior. The popular media uses sex to get ratings, not to accurately portray people's lives. The truth is that married people have more and better sex than singles do. But if you go by cultural myths, singles are having incredible, delicious sex that married couples only dream about. Focus on your relationship as it is right now and ask yourself if you'd like to make some changes. If you do, and especially if you want your sex life to have a bit more gusto, go for it.

☑ *Read books on how to add zing to your love life.* Especially if you have come to believe certain sexual myths, these books might clear the clutter from your head. Anyone can learn something new when it comes to sex.

☑ *Complete the sentence: "If I could change two things about my sex life they would be _____."* If you come up with answers quickly, chances are your partner will, too. And chances are some changes might improve the situation.

Keep in Mind

♡ No one's sex life is perfect all the time.

♡ Many people believe at least one false idea about lovemaking or sexuality.

♡ Happy couples don't "revolve" and do the same sexual things over and over. Instead, they "evolve" and adapt to each other's changing needs and desires.

Troubleshooter's Q&A: "Dear Dr. Coleman"

Curious about the kinds of issues many couples need help resolving? Having trouble knowing how to begin making improvements in your own marriage? This Troubleshooter's Q&A can shed some light.

Dear Dr. Coleman,

Help! We're definitely in a rut. I rarely see much of my spouse anymore. We're too busy with our jobs and the kids. By the end of the day we're too tired to do much of anything. I'm worried we will grow apart.

You're describing a problem common to many couples these days, even if they don't have children. Job demands for many people take up more and more of their time. I recommend you start with **Secret #1** and find a way to make small talk (that you must inevitably engage in at least some of the time) something you can take full advantage of. You must have at least twenty minutes a day of "couple time" that makes you feel connected. Breathing the same air does not qualify.

Then skip to **Secret #3** to learn how to have magical attentiveness. There are many ways you can connect and pay attention to each other that cost you very little time and energy—perfect for busy couples like yourselves.

If you haven't been connecting very well, then one or both of you may have some underlying resentments. **Secret #21** on hidden agendas might shed some light on any underlying issues.

Dear Dr. Coleman,
My spouse and I debate everything. If he says " night," I say "day." I'm very tired of all our arguing. But "giving in" doesn't feel right, either. Maybe we just see things differently and aren't compatible. What do you think?

It wouldn't surprise me if you are both firstborn children—or at least had responsible roles growing up—because you each think you know best. You're right; all that debating is not good. **Secret #17** discusses how to give up your need to always be right without feeling like you're caving in. You should also check out **Secret #22** to help you learn to de-escalate arguments. If your arguments escalate you might refuse to cooperate and yield on certain points—not because you sincerely believe you are right—but because you're hurt and angry that your partner is being inconsiderate or controlling.

Secret #28 discusses conversation killers. My guess is that you each have made your share of them. Finally, **Secret #5** tells you how to yield to your partner's wishes more often. That simple act (going along with your partner rather than being difficult) is highly predictive of a lasting and loving relationship. I'm not suggesting that you abandon your values. But I'm sure that if you look closely you'll see that you and your spouse often debate issues that are either not too important or that you could compromise on if you tried.

Dear Dr. Coleman,
Are all men animals? I swear my husband can't go ten minutes without thinking of sex. If I cuddle up to him he starts grabbing me. If I kiss him he starts grabbing me. If I say I'm going to bed he has an expression on his face similar to what my six-year-old had when I said we were going to Disney World. Is he oversexed or am I overreacting?

Get him to read **Secret #8** *ASAP!* While it's wonderful that he thinks you're attractive I sense that you're feeling more like a sexual object than a cherished spouse. My guess is he is putting most of his intimacy apples into the sex basket and has forgotten about the very important and nonsexual ways to improve intimacy. The chapter on supersizing intimacy (**Secret #11**) will give him some clear tips on what to do differently.

It also seems that you are like the majority of couples and have mismatched sexual desires. **Secret #20** talks about differences that can never get resolved (mismatched sexual desire leads the list) and describes how to manage those differences so the relationship can stay happy.

Dear Dr. Coleman,
My husband has a lot of hobbies that he really enjoys. But they keep him away from home too much. I rarely see him, and when I do, I don't feel all that connected to him since I've gotten used to spending

time alone. Is he being selfish with his outside interests? I tell him he is and he says the problem is that I don't have any interests of my own. Who's right?

A good relationship is a question of balance. Obviously you need to have both quality and quantity time together if the relationship is to be happy and long lasting. But personal hobbies are important, too. Anything one does that adds to a sense of creativity, relaxation, or achievement can have a positive impact on one's attitude. This, in turn, can benefit the marriage. If you are not involved in any personal hobbies you are like a lot of women. Women, more than men, will forgo personal interests if they interfere with marital or family functioning. Men are a bit less likely to do that.

I suggest you first take a hard look at your husband's observation that you have no personal hobbies. If that's true, you will or have already become more dependent on him for your happiness. Better to join a club or take a course or have a regular night out with friends than complain. Of course, if you do that, your husband needs to be willing to play with his schedule to accommodate to yours. There should be no double standards. (See **Secret #29.**)

Saying that, it wouldn't surprise me if his schedule has gotten out of hand and his priorities (you) are upside down. I suggest you discuss ways to spend more quality time together (read **Secret #11** on supersizing your intimacy levels) consistently. You might want a regular date night, for example. Or, you might agree to have at least twenty minutes together every day (see **Secret #1**) to boost overall warmth and goodwill.

The only way to really adjust to his not being around much is to start caring less. But that is not a good idea. The only way to continue to care about each other despite his hobbies is to make sure you do have regular, quality time together.

Dear Dr. Coleman,

My wife is too critical. She finds fault with me far too often, even over small things. When she has a complaint, she can't simply bring it up calmly but she has to bowl me over with an attack. I'm to the point where I avoid her as much as possible just to avoid an argument. This can't be a good thing.

I'm sure if I asked her she would tell me that her complaints are very legitimate and that she yells at or attacks you because you have not listened to her in the past. My guess is that you have both gotten trapped in a vicious cycle: The more you avoid her, the more angry she feels; the more angry she feels, the more she finds fault with you and attacks you; the more she attacks you, the more you avoid her.

Please read **Secrets #5, 7, 20, 21, 23,** and **28**. They should be your starting point. Those secrets address the ways conversations get crazy and harmful and they show how to repair conversations that have gone off track. Your wife must be willing to look at her role in the perpetuation of your problems (**Secret #7**) and realize that while her anger might be legitimate, her use of anger is hindering progress. **Secret #23** talks about how to reduce one's inner agitation, especially during conflict. I think you both could benefit from that chapter. She displays agitation by yelling and attacking, and you reveal your agitation by your need to withdraw to calm down.

Still, if you two have many positive interactions (Part One of this book is all about increasing positive interactions) then the negatives won't be so destructive.

Dear Dr. Coleman,
I want to feel more committed to my spouse but some days I contemplate moving on. How can I be sure we can be happy together? Maybe ending this relationship and starting over with someone else is the best way to go. Any thoughts?

The more extreme your problems (abuse, alcoholism, drug addiction, gambling) then the more "moving on" might be a better idea, especially if you have tried hard to overcome these issues together and not succeeded. If the problems you have have always been there and are part of your partner's personality, they are less likely to change. If you have children, you are undoubtedly worried about the impact that splitting up will have on them. There is no way to predict on an individual basis. However, research findings indicate that kids are better off if their parents stay together (unhappily) when the parents are not arguing much and there is nothing toxic happening, such as alcohol addiction or abuse. If there is a lot of fighting, the kids will probably fare better if the parents split up. When a couple does separate or divorce, kids fare best when the parents are cooperative with parenting and the noncustodial parent (usually Dad) has regular visits. Still, you might want to read **Secrets #4, 13,** and **14**. There are ways for couples to boost their commitment. Also, if you can find a sacred purpose to your marriage (**Secret #13**) you might rethink your plans.

Starting over with a clean slate sounds positive in theory, but it's rarely easy in practice. First, if you are contributing to relationship problems you will probably do so again in your next relationship. Second, your new partner might be better than your current partner in some ways but perhaps not as good in other ways. "Trading up" is not always a guarantee. If you have had a series of unsuccessful relationships, you might want to talk to a counselor and see if there are any insights you can gain about yourself. You might be overlooking your faults or might be choosing the wrong person time and again.

Finally, the decision to move on depends also on how complicated your life is. If you have a career and no kids and the property distribution is a no-brainer, and if you keep hitting your head against the wall in the relationship and can't sustain any kind of happiness, you might find that moving on makes sense.

Dear Dr. Coleman,

I got home from a very long day at work and just sat down to eat something when my four-year-old son wanted a snack. My wife asked me to get it for him. I said, "Why can't you do it?" She got mad at me. We always fight about such things. I work hard and I don't think she appreciates all I do. I know she works hard, too, but is it too much to expect her to care for my son when I'm trying to eat dinner after a long day?

The short answer is: Yes. It is too much to expect. I'm not saying you should always be the one who is inconvenienced.

I'm saying that the scenario you're describing is commonplace and that trying to compete for the title of "Most Tired and Overworked" will not serve you or your marriage. I'm betting that you each are tired and you each are overworked. That being the case, neither one of you has clarity of judgment when you are convinced that you are more overloaded than the other one is. When you sit down to dinner after a long day you are fully aware of all you had to go through during the day. But you are not fully aware of all your spouse had to go through. It is presumptuous to think that you are more tired or more entitled to a break than she is. And even if you can objectively prove that you did more work than she did all day, does that automatically entitle you to call out the trump card and say "You do it!" when you don't want to do a certain task? No it doesn't. Marriages don't work that way. Sometimes you do for the other even if you don't think it's fair. You do it out of love and friendship and goodwill.

Secret #20 should be required reading for you and your spouse. It addresses how to handle recurrent problems. The problem you describe is what I call a recurrent problem since there will never be a perfect, "once and for all" solution. You also should read **Secret #4** on how to be good friends. Good friends would understand when they have to be inconvenienced. It isn't your son's fault that he wants a snack, nor is it your wife's fault that she doesn't want to give it to him. For that matter it isn't your fault that you don't want to give him a snack. The situation simply "is." And it must be handled every time it and others like it come up. Will you choose to handle all those situations by debating and arguing? Or will you choose to be a friend to your spouse, a friend who is willing to be inconvenienced a little more than you think you should be?

By the way, **Secret #17** on how to reduce your need to be right might also be of interest to both you and your wife.

Dear Dr. Coleman,
I've been married to my husband for three months. I was given the advice to keep both eyes open before marriage and keep one eye closed after marriage. I guess that means I shouldn't expect perfection. But if I really don't like something my spouse does should I speak up and insist it be changed? Shouldn't I learn to be tolerant?

Read **Secret #19**. Research shows that women who accommodated to objectionable behavior by their husbands early on in the marriage (they hoped he would change or the behaviors would simply go away over time) were not happy several years later. The happier wives spoke up soon about things they really disliked. Don't nitpick. Choose your battles. Can you really put up with the behavior? Is it more of a nuisance or is it really objectionable? If it's objectionable, nip it in the bud. You will both be happier for it later.

Dear Dr. Coleman,
Whenever my wife and I have an argument she eventually tells her friends about it and also my mother-in-law. I hate that. I believe our personal life should remain private. She disagrees. What should we do?

At first blush I agree with you. All else being equal, it's better that your wife at least keeps the specifics to herself. It's especially risky to speak ill of you to her mother. However, she might be confiding in others because she is at her wit's end trying to work things out with you. Have you tried to be cooperative? When you argue or disagree, are you stubborn and difficult or can you yield somewhat to her concerns (see **Secret #5**)? Sometimes people who tend to be very controlling in their relationships use the privacy argument as a legitimate way to continue to be controlling. Has your wife ever told you that you were controlling? Has she complained that things have to always go your way or that the relationship isn't fair? Are there double standards (**Secret #29**)? If any of these apply then it's not a simple matter of getting your wife to keep your marital issues private.

Dear Dr. Coleman,
My wife is suspicious of me because I have female coworkers. I've never been unfaithful and never have given her a reason to think I'm unfaithful. But if I go to lunch with any female coworkers I get the third degree. I'm tired of her accusations. What should I do?

First, be honest. Is it true that you've never given her reason to mistrust you? **Secret #25** has some important insights. If you are innocent, then your marriage is in serious trouble unless your wife is willing to examine her issues more closely. Having to defend your innocence time and again will drain you of any emotional connection to her. More insidiously, you run the risk of lying or being secretive about things that you believe your wife will misinterpret. If she catches you in the lie or secret, she will then have "proof" that you cannot be trusted but it will be a scenario that she herself helped to bring about.

Perhaps **Secret #21** on uncovering hidden agendas might be of help. Odds are pretty high that your wife has felt betrayed in the past and you are on the receiving end of her insecurities. Also, giving the benefit of the doubt (**Secret #2**) and becoming better friends (**Secret #4**) might help.

Dear Dr. Coleman,
My marriage is a complete mess. I'm not even sure we love each other anymore. But we don't want to end it. Where do we begin?

You need to increase your emotional connection without doing anything that can start an argument or make one of you want to pull away. Begin with **Secret #1**. It teaches you how to have nonthreatening intimate moments by the use of ordinary small talk. Then read **Secrets #2** through **5**. They're at the top of the *30 Secrets* list for a reason: They're powerful. Couples who aren't connecting don't give each other the benefit of the doubt. Neutral behaviors are interpreted negatively and positive behaviors are interpreted cynically. You must begin thinking differently about one another. You need to pay attention to each other (**Secret #3**) in ways that don't come across as pushy, demanding, or needy. Nurturing each other (**Secret #4**) is essential. That includes thoughtful gestures and acts of kindness and consideration. Finally, start yielding to one another's wishes whenever you can (**Secret #5**). I'm not saying you must go along with whatever your spouse wants. You have a right to disagree. But chances are you two are on automatic pilot when it comes to being uncooperative and stopped listening attentively a long time ago. Cooperate when you can and stop squabbling over small stuff.

Lastly, you must decrease any negative interactions as much as possible. **Secrets #16** through **30** are all about the negative attitudes and actions that must be reduced. The sobering truth is that one negative interaction will cost you at least five (and probably ten) positive interactions. In other words, you have to have five times as many positive interactions as negative in order to have a reasonably satisfying relationship. When a marriage is a "mess," there are too many negatives and virtually no positives. You have to reverse that trend quickly.

Dear Dr. Coleman,
If you could give newly married couples only a few pieces of advice, what would you say?

I'd say that their marriage will bring out the best in each of them if they always lean in the direction of harboring goodwill and possessing a willingness to make sacrifices. I'd remind them that when disagreements occur there will be no outside authority to determine what they should do. They must therefore find ways to settle or manage their differences in a manner that doesn't create resentment. It's okay to complain but not okay to attack. Finally, I'd suggest that both partners examine their past and make a list of the key hurts or fears they endured. Is there a theme? How do they try to protect themselves from being hurt like that again? How does that manner of protection affect their marriage? Too often spouses get nailed for causing injuries that began with earlier relationships. Be willing to cut your spouse some slack.

I'd also encourage couples to foster their spiritual side. Asking, "What can I do to achieve the highest good?" or "What would God want us to do?" can help them figure out the steps they need to take in many situations.

Dear Dr. Coleman,
Is marital happiness really a legitimate goal? Isn't it hard to always be happy? Perhaps the best one can hope for is contentment with the occasional happiness thrown in. What do you think?

As I said at the outset, happiness is not a quality we can obtain directly. It is a by-product of the way you lead your life. Sure, contentment is a fine way to feel and I imagine it's better than discontentment. But most couples don't get married to be content. They want to be happy together. I believe that couples that are happily married act in ways that are distinctly different from couples that are less than happy. And those ways are outlined in this book. Set your sights higher than they are now. Happiness is not an unreasonable goal. Of course, life events (such as financial or health setbacks) can make you temporarily unhappy. But it's nice to know that your marriage is not only sound, it's thriving. A thriving marriage can help you get through even the most difficult times.

Bibliography

Alexander, Susanne M., & Farnsworth, Craig A. *Pure Gold: Encouraging Character Qualities in Marriage.* Cleveland: Marriage Transformation L.L.C., 2004.

Bader, E., & Peterson, P. *In Quest of the Mythical Mate.* New York: Bruner/ Mazel, 1988.

Bergman, Joel. On Odd Days and On Even Days: Rituals Used in Strategic Therapy. In L. Wolberg's & M. Araonson's (eds.) *Group and Family Therapy,* New York: Brunner/Mazel, 1983.

Coleman, Paul. *25 Stupid Mistakes Couples Make.* Chicago: Contemporary Books, 2001.

———. *How to Say It™ for Couples: Communicating with Tenderness, Openness, and Honesty.* Paramus, New Jersey: Prentice Hall, 2002.

———. *The Forgiving Marriage: Overcoming Anger and Resentment and Rediscovering Each Other.* Chicago: Contemporary Books, 1989.

De Angelis, Barbara. *What Women Want Men to Know.* New York: Hyperion, 2001.

Driscoll, Richard. *The Binds That Tie.* Lexington, MA: Lexington Books, 1991.

Enright, Robert D. *Forgiveness Is a Choice: A Step-by-Step Process for Resolving Anger and Restoring Hope.* Washington, DC: American Psychological Association, 2001.

Gottman, John. *The Marriage Clinic: A Scientifically Based Marital Therapy.* New York: W. W. Norton and Company, 1999.

Greeley, Andrew. *Faithful Attraction: Discovering Intimacy, Love, and Fideltiy in American Marriages.* New York: Tor, 1991.

Larson, J., Crane, R., & Smith, C. Morning and Night Couples: The Effect of Wake and Sleep Patterns on Marital Adjustment. *Journal of Marital and Family Therapy, 17*(1), 1991, 53-65.

Markman, Howard. PREP: Preventing Marital Distress Through Constructive Arguing. *Workshop presented at Annual Convention of the American Association for Marriage and Family Therapy,* Dallas, 1991.

Mellman, M., Lazarus, E., and Rivlin, A. Family Time, Family Values. In David Blankenhorn's, Steven Bayone's, and Jean Elshtains's (eds.) *Rebuilding the Nest: New Commitment to the American Family,* 1990, 52, 904-912.

O'Hanlon, W., & Weiner-Davis, M. *In Search of Solutions: A New Direction in Psychotherapy.* New York: W. W. Norton and Company, 1989.

Real, Terrence. *How Can I Get Through to You: Closing the Intimacy Gap Between Men and Women.* New York: Fireside, 2002.

Tannen, Deborah. *You Just Don't Understand: Men and Women in Conversation.* New York: HarperCollins, 1990.

Weiner Davis, Michele. *The Sex-Starved Marriage: Boosting Your Marriage Libido.* New York: Simon & Schuster, 2003.

Wile, Daniel. *After the Fight: A Night in the Life of a Couple.* New York: Guilford, 1993.

————. *After the Honeymoon: How Conflicts Can Improve Your Relationship.* New York: Wiley, 1988.

Index